TARTUFFE

and

THE WOULD-BE GENTLEMAN

MOLIÈRE

TARTUFFE

&

THE WOULD-BE GENTLEMAN

Translated by
H. BAKER *and* J. MILLER

With an Introduction by
HENRI PEYRE

and Illustrations by
SERGE IVANOFF

THE HERITAGE PRESS
New York

CONTENTS

Introduction

In the whole range of comedy, from Aristophanes down to the present theatre of the absurd, there are very few plays, if any, whose power and appeal can rival, in universality and in perennial youth, Molière's *Tartuffe* and *The Would-Be Gentleman*. They were first performed within two years of each other, *Tartuffe* in its revised version and after arduous tribulations on February 5, 1669, the other on October 14, 1670. In February 1673, one week after he had been taken mortally ill off-stage while acting *The Imaginary Invalid*, Molière died.

The ten years which elapsed between the death of Pascal in 1662 and that of Molière remain the most glorious decade in French literature. Louis XIV stood surrounded by magnificence and asserting French military and cultural pre-eminence; but the rigid formality of Versailles, the piety which Mme de Maintenon was later to impose upon the French Court, had not yet prevailed. The unruliness of the Three Musketeers, the violence of the restless, dueling nobility, the civil disorders of the Fronde were still fairly recent. Theatrical audiences were weary of heroism and yearned for psychological realism; they well knew that passion sways men and women more potently than the desire for order and the Cartesian nostalgia for reason.

The comedian Jouvet, who played Molière most brilliantly in our century, well remarked in a lecture in 1937: "Molière, who has been labeled the champion of reason, is the man who best understood and sensed what unreason is; his theatre, in which some superficial commentators would hail the triumph of reason, is above all else the realm of that marvelous unreason called poetry."

Molière, nearing forty, had barely returned from his long tour of the French provinces; in 1659 he had taken Paris by storm with *The Precious Damsels*. In *The School for Women*, in 1662, he mocked the claims of the males (especially males who, like him, marry much younger wives, expecting that henceforth these creatures will be submissive enough to see life and love only through the eyes of their wiser husbands). The ten commandments of obedience to the husband, Lord and Master, could not but strike contemporaries as a parody of Christian teaching. From that day on, people of piety (they were legion in a deeply religious France) and the falsely devout were determined to oppose the blasphemous author. They soon found their chance.

The seventeenth century endeavored to impose stability upon a country which had been torn for a hundred years by religious wars, and to restore Catholicism to its high estate after the excesses and unruliness that the Reformation had denounced. In France—where the order of the Jesuits had been founded by the Spaniard Ignatius of Loyola in 1534, where the Oratorians were created in 1611 and the Sulpicians in 1650, where Jansenism grew after Jansenius himself had died in 1638—there had been born in 1627 a less illustrious but very active congregation, the Company of the Holy Sacrament. Pious men belonging to that Company, often also athirst for authority over souls, went to live in the homes of middle-class people, as parsons often did in the households of British squires in the eighteenth century. The visitor dispensed advice on morals and on the children's education; he kept a jealous vigil over the behavior of the wife, and reported to the husband if he perceived anything untoward in her resistance to temptations. If the Company had had their way, they would gladly have closed all theatres, as the Puritans did in England in 1642. Occasionally their devoutness looked rather like bigotry and served as a cover for lust.

Molière did not draw the inspiration for *Tartuffe* from contemporary incidents, but he composed it in the midst of controversies. On the one side was the religious party at the Court, with the Queen Mother, Anne of Austria; the young Queen, Marie-Thérèse; and even the wealthy financier Fouquet, not yet fallen from his lofty position and a patron of the Company of the Holy Sacrament. In 1663–64 they were watching the young King fall in love with Mlle de La Vallière and ready to blame the general dissolution of manners on the august example. Louis XIV himself had evinced his sympathy for Molière and consented in 1664 to serve as godfather to the comedian's first-born child, appropriately christened Louis. The same year that he ordered lavish festivities ostensibly for the Queen but, as everyone knew, for Mlle de La Vallière, three acts of *Tartuffe* were performed and the play was applauded.

A cabal was soon launched by the pious party; Molière was pictured as a demon deserving to burn at the stake as a foretaste of the fire of hell. Molière withstood the outcry but changed Tartuffe's name to Panuphle and the character's clerical dress for that of a man of the world. Still the Archbishop of Paris forbade the faithful, under pain of excommunication, to attend any performance of the play, and it was soon altogether prohibited. Molière appealed to the King, who after some delay, during which Molière had attacked bigotry even more violently in *Don Juan,* allowed public performances. *Tartuffe* was now given to packed houses and wildly acclaimed.

Still, the vituperations of the ecclesiastics lost none of their vehemence. The most eloquent Jesuit preacher of the day, Bourdaloue, lashed out against "those damnable inventions contrived to humiliate worthy people and to render all of them suspect." Bossuet's solemn voice thundered: "Woe unto you that laugh now, for ye shall weep!" Even in our own age, François Mauriac, whose novels are far from resembling innocuous Sunday School stories, has indicted Molière for his belief in the goodness of nature and of common sense, and for making such fun of Orgon, who after all is a passionate and genuine Christian. Molière's punishment, concludes Mauriac, was to live with sadness and remorse, while Pascal the believer was favored with "tears of joy."

II

The *Tartuffe* controversy is one of the *causes célèbres* of French literature. Molière suffered from it, for scurrilous attacks were directed at his wife and at her probable infidelities. Molière, however, would not yield. Courtier, diplomat, administrator of a theatrical company always in need of the King's favor, Molière had to be flexible and resourceful, and he was. But on the rightful claim of the theatre to present the gravest and boldest subjects on the stage, he would not yield. In *Tartuffe* he was defending the comedian's profession, the freedom of the comic actor to ridicule even his audiences and the powerful people around. It is a passionate play, with a vibrant message embodied in it—but it is also a superb work of art and, serious as the issue is at times, it is also a great comedy, one that arouses laughter and is well calculated to fulfill its purpose: *castigat ridendo mores.* Hypocrisy has survived *Tartuffe* as casuistry has survived Pascal's *Provincial Letters*; but it has never since dared display itself quite so blatantly.

The exposition is masterly; Goethe never ceased to admire it. It takes us no longer to the public square of the Italian comedy and of *The School for Women,* where acquaintances casually meet, but inside a middle-class home. The atmosphere of a bourgeois drama is at once created. The whole family, bitterly divided over Tartuffe's intrusion, is vividly presented.

In the second act, an interlude between the superb exposition and Tartuffe's long-awaited arrival, the action slows down. Some comic relief was needed, and it is provided by Dorine's sharp repartee with her master and by a fuller portrayal of Orgon's almost unbelievable gullibility.

Tartuffe's entry early in Act III is one of the great feats of the comic theatre, and after the long-built-up expectation it invariably stages a triumph for great players of the role. He audaciously boasts about his good works and his ascetic penance, pretends to be scandalized by Dorine's décolleté, and does not conceal his eagerness when the servant announces that Orgon's wife Elmire wishes to talk with him.

In her presence Tartuffe becomes all smiles and mellowness, he is a master of unctuous seduction. When Elmire attempts to set the conversation on the subject of Mariane's marriage to him, Tartuffe embarks upon an eloquent declaration in two long tirades, just as Phèdre will do, a decade or so later, in her avowals to her stepson. He shifts the language of the mystics onto the plane of carnal love, juggles masterfully with ambiguities, and, in his quality of a pious man, hints at the security he can offer: discretion, love without scandal, and pleasure without fear. Orgon's son Damis, who has strategically been placed by the servant in an adjoining closet, then rushes out and upbraids Elmire. She restrains his impetuousness. Elmire has obviously heard such declarations before and feels able to deal with men by herself.

After Act III the comedy briefly borders on tragedy. Orgon, irate against Damis' distrust of Tartuffe, curses him in a declamatory gesture worthy of a picture by Greuze. Religious fanaticism has made Orgon obdurate and cruel. Tartuffe's arrogance now knows no bounds. Elmire will resort to the most convincing of devices, since her foolish husband, for whom her scorn is hardly disguised, refuses to see the light by himself. Aware of her power over Tartuffe, she will bring him in and lead him to a complete unmasking of his feelings for her: a mixture of lechery, admiration, and perhaps also of genuine love. She pretends, using Tartuffe's own roundabout and poetical language, not to have been insensitive to his advances. Tartuffe requests "palpable evidence" of her affection: our mystic is also a realist. He offers to make all the arrangements with Heaven which might soothe her scruples: he had gone to school to the casuists whom Pascal had vilified. As for the husband, Tartuffe does not conceal the scorn in which he holds Orgon, whom he boasts of having taught to disbelieve what he sees.

Orgon at last emerges from under the table. He cannot even expel

Tartuffe, since he has signed the gift of his house away to the hypocrite. All's well that ends well, however, and the dénouement, which saves Orgon from the consequences of his stubborn and perverse silliness, is effected by an emissary of the King, who redresses the wrongs and takes the impostor to prison.

A few cantankerous or supercilious critics, reading the play in their studies and scrutinizing every detail, have taken issue with the relief provided by this dénouement. On the stage, the illogic is readily accepted and the happy ending in no way detracts from the audience's pleasure. If the visual requirements of the theatre are taken into account (and Molière, actor and director, always wrote with a specific view to staging), *Tartuffe* has a masterly structure. It unfolds with suspense and moments of relief, produces almost tragic emotions, touches—more than Shakespeare often does in his poetical comedies—on the seriousness of life when scratched beneath the surface, and takes place on several levels with equal mastery.

Molière himself brought out the farcical aspects of Orgon's character in his interpretation of the part. For upon Orgon's asinine gullibility the whole play hinges. Some features of the silly, infatuated fool of the Italian comedy and of the complacent cuckold linger in Orgon. He is ludicrous; but is he so very exaggerated? We have all known such men, literally possessed by one fixed idea, egocentric and monstrously selfish, tyrannizing their own families as Orgon does through Tartuffe.

A French critic has noted that with only two letters changed, the name of Orgon becomes that of Argan, the "imaginary invalid." Argan is ridiculous and selfish, ready to force his daughter to marry a doctor, and no other, because he is afraid of disease and of death. Orgon wants naïvely to be sure of his own salvation, and he would sacrifice all his family to that sole purpose. Religion, narrowly conceived, controls him, and it has made a fool of him. Only outside interventions, and a seduction scene that is coolly, masterfully orchestrated by his wife under his very nose, can dissuade him; but is not his stupidity incurable? "Sometimes the wicked man undergoes a change for the better," remarked Anatole France, "but the fool never does." How will Orgon behave three or five years later? What love or esteem will Elmire feel for him? The later life of dramatic characters who survive the dénouement is ever the most tantalizing subject for our imagination.

Orgon serves as the pivot of the play, but Elmire has too much self-mastery to revolve around him. She says little, she listens, sure of her purpose and of her sway over Tartuffe—over any suitor, perhaps. Molière, who was entrusting the part to his own young wife, left much of what the inquisitive playgoer might wish to know of Elmire in a mysterious shade. Is she another frigid coquette, like Célimène, but with a less biting tongue? Her mother-in-law's insidious allusions to Elmire's fondness for balls and entertainments might rest on some actual observation. She clearly is not religious and her virtue is not of the intractable kind which would in advance discourage any rival of her monomaniac of a husband, who must never have brought her much happiness, physical or other.

Tartuffe, who appears relatively seldom and delivers only two or three lengthy speeches, is nevertheless one of the most admired character-portrayals in literature. We know him through the description, the hatred and fear, or the inordinate infatuation, of others. Molière, well aware that only a tenuous line differentiates the exteriors of false devoutness and genuine piety, was forced to dot his i's; he exaggerates the outward manifestations of Tartuffe's piety, his praying, kneeling, sighing, and lamenting his unworthiness. The audience would not have forgiven the comic writer if it had been taken in by a portrayal of normal piety, to discover later that the mask only concealed a villain.

Yet Tartuffe is not all black. He is—Molière forcefully underlines it—an impostor and a hypocrite, but his creator was far too subtle a psychologist to leave it at that. Was Tartuffe once virtuous? How was he converted to his career of "resident saint" and where did he learn the mystical language which he masterfully wields? Did he become religious in order to curb the greed of his flesh and to obey an authority from above, being unable to impose any rule of restraint upon himself? Repulsive, farcical, Tartuffe occasionally is. But like all living characters, he is not all of a piece. He exerts a strange fascination, as do a number of charlatans, salesmen, comedians, politicians, lecturers. Tartuffe today would probably no longer select the church as the ground for his adventures and self-aggrandizement; his field would be public relations in the oil industry or in communications, or venal politics. But he would be the same dynamic, aggressive upstart unhampered by any scruples. The same mixture of willful deceit and sincere self-deception characterizes his many descendants in our midst.

Molière had to muster up all his audacity to attack religious hypocrisy, for—unlike miserliness, pedantry, coquetry, medicine even, or cuckoldry—a whole social institution was being called in question. Molière was no Voltaire. He did not profess anticlericalism, then unborn. He was scourging the defects of those who were duped by the outward show of piety and by religious intolerance. He probably was but a tepid Christian himself, as was Shakespeare when, in *Measure for Measure* and *Twelfth Night,* he upheld the claims of the theatre against the Puritans. But the good and the evil are inextricably blended in human motives. Some of the truest religious men have been fanatics. The Company of the Holy Sacrament accomplished many good works.

Bourdaloue asked a relevant question when he remarked, apropos of such denunciations of religious hypocrisy: "In tearing off the mask, does not comedy run the risk of scratching the face?" A placid, neutral, reasonable faith, such as Elmire and Cléante, the reasoner in the play, probably stand for, would hardly win converts. It would not guide life or inspire a code of ethics. It is the religion of many of our contemporaries in an age which Malraux has called the aftermath of the absolute. Molière, or any comic writer—and he outranges every one of them—cannot aspire to the sovereign universality of a Shakespeare whose dramatic irony understands —hence forgives—Iago and Othello, Edgar and Edmund alike. Molière had to hate vice in order to castigate it and to hope to correct at least a part of his audience. He was fighting the foes of his own theatre, of sincerity in literature, and of honesty in life.

Wherever and whenever *Tartuffe* is performed and read today, the same battle is being waged by implication: against the hypocrisy of statesmen and politicians, the befogged jargon of our experts, the pompousness of many psychologists and analysts of what in Greek used to designate the soul, the display of patriotism and civic conscience that often serves as a cloak for social climbing or for commercial benefits.

Molière died without benefit of clergy, and the Church consented grudgingly to bury him only in the plot reserved for suicides and stillbirths. His rebellious spirit has not lost its élan and its edge after three hundred years. "If Molière were alive today," wrote the best recent critic of his work, the Englishman W. G. Moore, "writing with the same clear vision and unthinking disregard of contemporary verities, the most revolutionary plays of our own time would seem but a thin cackling by comparison with the broad laughter of his comic genius."

III

Goethe, who every year reread a few plays of Molière with enhanced delight, is often quoted for his pronouncement that works of circumstance can also be very great works. *The Would-Be Gentleman* was literally composed on order from the King and it had to be a "comédie-ballet," with music and dancing, a "divertimento" in which a gallicized Italian like Lulli (who played the part of the Mufti) excelled. The assignment might well have daunted any author who was not endowed with Molière's astonishing facility. For that kind of play had to end as a masquerade, and the body of the work could thus not, as in *Tartuffe* or *Don Juan*, border on tragedy. The characters were not expected to be profound, or to undergo a harmonious development; even more than in most comedies they had to be static and to be revealed in several of their facets through diversified episodes. And naturally such comedy, on a less exalted plane than *Tartuffe* or *The Misanthrope*, would be in prose, like *Don Juan*, and depend upon familiar, pungent dialogue.

Molière set to work as soon as the order for the King's "divertimento" was conveyed to him. He was a friend of Lulli, but could not help sensing that the Italian entertainer and musician—an indefatigable dancer, supple, hale, younger than Molière, untouched by the premonitions of disease which Molière must have felt three years before his death—was also his rival and not above plotting against him for the royal favor. He utilized a few stock scenes on subjects which he had already tested and through which he was sure to provoke laughter: a nobleman's skill at putting off his creditors, a marriage of two sincere and naïve lovers crossed by the selfishness of one of the parents, a saucy maid shrugging off her master's foolishness. But he welded those scenes with superb felicitousness into an animated whole. He took advantage of his public's passing interest in Turkish subjects, but his comedy is a universal one; versions of it in forty languages have aroused laughter, and it has lost none of its splendor and sharpness when transposed to the screen.

The first performance of *The Would-Be Gentleman* took place at Chambord on October 14, 1670. Six weeks later it was given for the general public. It satirized the dishonesty of some members of the nobility and the vain snobbery of the middle class when it apes the nobility. Once again Molière was staging a frontal attack upon his own public, and scoring a resounding victory. Both the Court and Paris applauded, and the box-office receipts were gratifying. The play has remained a favorite with all who like comedy and who can admire the truth of its portrayal of living individuals. It contains excellent social satire.

The bourgeoisie was fast ascending during the heyday of the French monarchy. Louis XIV systematically distrusted the nobles, who had chafed under Richelieu's yoke and attempted to weaken the infant Sun King's power during the Fronde. He resorted to a number of the bourgeois for his more competent and more flexible civil servants. Since the nobility was not supposed to engage in trade or in professions, financiers, lawyers, men of affairs came from the middle class, grew rich, and eventually expected to have their well-provided daughters marry members of the impoverished nobility. Writers like Furetière, the very original author of *Le Roman Bourgeois* (1666), then Molière, a little later La Bruyère, Lesage, Dancourt, were among the shrewdest observers of that great social phenomenon: the ascent and self-assertion of the French middle class. Like much of French literature, *The Would-Be Gentleman* is an apt piece of social criticism.

The plot is almost nonexistent. This is not what the French categorize as a *comédie d'intrigue,* with bewildering vicissitudes and an elaborate contrivance of suspense. There is action and the succession of the scenes is lively, with no slowing of the tempo, but no attempt at making credible what is destined to end in a riotous fantasy. As early as the second scene we see Monsieur Jourdain, complacent, ingenuous, eager, appear among the teachers whom he has engaged. Unlike Harpagon or Tartuffe, he arouses immediate sympathy in spite of his absurdities. Molière had, however, to take care that the audience would not be carried away by too strong a sympathy with the vain upstart whose absurdity he was going to expose. We are told nothing of his past, of the hard work and the business skill he must have displayed in order to become rich, of his poverty as a child, perhaps, and his secret mortification at having failed to receive a decent education. A comic character, naïvely ridiculous, about whom we would know too much, would quickly bring us to identify ourselves with his growth; but, to remain entertaining, he must be presented to us ready-made, as it were, congealed in his present personality, rigidified by age, and stultified by one all-devouring and fixed idea.

But we feel no dislike for Monsieur Jourdain. He has many younger brothers among us today, in Europe as in America, even more in this country where many a man in trade or manufacturing, who has started from the bottom and been deprived of education and of refinement, decides one day to study good manners, to learn about music and philosophy, become a patron of the arts, and would not mind marrying his daughter to some German baron or Italian prince. Rousseau, a plebeian himself and a self-made man, was among the first to remark that Monsieur Jourdain is far more likable than the nobleman who swindles him so blatantly. He blamed the immorality of the author, and of the theatregoer, for making us laugh at Dorante's sly cleverness and at Monsieur Jourdain as his simple but generous dupe. As for Dorimène, she hardly seems to understand what is going on, and her condition as a gentlewoman and as a young widow has not sharpened her perceptiveness. Indeed the nobility does not emerge unscathed from Molière's social satire in this play, or in others.

Molière was a social satirist and a moralist only secondarily, and all the more effective thereby. First of all, he had to arouse laughter in his audience; and he had been right when, in the *Critique of the School for Women,* he asserted that such a task was infinitely harder than that of any tragic poet—or, we would now add, of any novelist. He could not portray Monsieur Jourdain in the perspective of his life, in "his becoming," as we put it today, or even as too concrete an individuality. He had to be a type, therefore to be depicted only on the surface of himself, and to be presented as seen by others who are aware of his ludicrous foibles. In this respect the opening scene, with the several teachers of music, dancing, fencing, and philosophy (modestly starting from phonetics and elements of grammar) vying with each other in boastfulness and greed, is a masterpiece. Every one of these dispensers of the arts is inflated with professional conceit and convinced, in his stiffness and arrogance, that he holds the key to some deep mysteries into which the simple Monsieur Jourdain may be initiated.

Madame Jourdain, with her sharp common sense, her gift of repartee, her attachment to the shopkeepers' class to which she is proud of belonging, her dry and shrewd unconcern for the glitter of the nobility and for the dis-

honesty which she associates with it, is one of Molière's admirable secondary
characters. Many a Frenchwoman whom we may observe to this very day
sitting at the counter in her shop, exchanging pithy, proverbial sayings with
the customers, treating all men—husbands in particular—as simple, over-
grown children, reminds us of that good, sensible, clamorous wife of the
lower middle class, proud of her standard of honesty.

The Would-Be Gentleman—unlike *Don Juan*, which owed its original theme
to Spain; unlike *The Miser*, whose debt to Plautus was considerable—is as
purely French a comedy as Molière ever composed. Its laughter is sane,
popular in its sources, genuine, never bitter, never wry or strained as in the
contemporary theatre of the absurd where we are constantly asked to contemplate the ludicrousness of the human condition. The ballet which concludes it leads us to accept the dénouement as falling within the poetical
logic of a play which constituted a vivid picture of a middle-class family: it
preserves the hilariousness of the play and the illusion that the greatest gift
of a comic writer to his audience is to enable it to see itself, and even its own
foibles or its own misfortunes, humorously and objectively. The late Raimu,
the film actor who interpreted Monsieur Jourdain for the Comédie Française,
so endowed that well-meaning and foolish bourgeois with a childish naïveté,
a disarming gullibility, an earnest intent to study dancing steps, good manners, phonetics, and even poetry, that he became forever a touching character in his very ridiculousness. After Molière himself and Coquelin the
younger, who had also played the role, the assignment of Monsieur Jourdain
to the most gifted comic actors of France may well dampen the audacity of
any of them.

The Turkish vogue that served as a pretext for the play, after an Ottoman
ambassador had vexed the King by remaining unimpressed and bored by
the luxury and majesty of Louis XIV's Court, has gone the way of all vogues.
The human substance of the play and its power to arouse laughter and joy in
us live on. In our present age, so fond of wallowing in its anxiety and ob-
sessed by its rediscovery of tragedy and its conviction that anguish is its lot
and its privilege, nothing in literature can help us restore a balanced view of
ourselves as richly as Molière's plays.

HENRI PEYRE

TARTUFFE

or

THE HYPOCRITE

ACTORS

MME PERNELLE   *mother to Orgon*

ORGON   *husband to Elmire*

ELMIRE   *wife to Orgon*

DAMIS   *son to Orgon*

MARIANE   *daughter to Orgon*

VALÈRE   *in love with Mariane*

CLÉANTE   *brother-in-law to Orgon*

TARTUFFE   *a hypocrite*

DORINE   *waiting-maid to Mariane*

M. LOYAL   *a bailiff*

A POLICE OFFICER

FLIPOTE   *Madame Pernelle's maid*

The scene is Paris, in Orgon's house

ACT I

Madame Pernelle, Elmire, Mariane, Damis, Cléante, Dorine, Flipote

Mme PERNELLE

Come Flipote, let's be gone, that I may get rid of them.

ELMIRE

You walk so fast that one has much ado to follow you.

Mme PERNELLE

Stay, daughter, stay; come no farther; this is all needless ceremony.

ELMIRE

We only acquit ourselves of our duty to you; but pray, mother, what makes you in such haste to leave us?

Mme PERNELLE

Because I can't endure to see such management, and nobody takes any care to please me. I leave your house, I tell you, very ill edified; my instructions are all contradicted. You show no respect for anything amongst you, every one talks aloud there, and the house is a perfect Dover Court.

DORINE

If—

Mme PERNELLE

You are, sweetheart, a noisy and impertinent Abigail, and mighty free of your advice on all occasions.

DAMIS

But—

Mme PERNELLE

In short, you are a fool, child; 'tis I tell you so, who am your grandmother; and I have told my son your father, a hundred times, that you would become a perfect rake and would be nothing but a plague to him.

MARIANE

I fancy—

Mme PERNELLE

Good-lack, sister of his, you act the prude, and look as if butter would not melt in your mouth; but still waters, they say, are always deepest, and under your sly airs you carry on a trade I don't at all approve of.

ELMIRE

But mother—

Mme PERNELLE

By your leave, daughter, your conduct is absolutely wrong in everything; you ought to set them a good example, and their late mother managed 'em much better. You are a sorry economist, and what I can't endure, dress like any princess. She who desires only to please her husband, daughter, needs not so much finery.

CLÉANTE

But madame, after all—

Mme PERNELLE

As for you, sir, her brother, I esteem you very much, I love and respect you; but yet, were I in my son's her husband's place, I should earnestly entreat you not to come within our doors. You are always laying down rules of life that good people should never follow. I talk a little freely to you, but 'tis my humour; I never chew upon what I have at heart.

DAMIS

Your Monsieur Tartuffe is a blessed soul, no doubt—

Mme PERNELLE

He's a good man, and should be listened to; I can't bear, with patience, to hear him cavilled at by such a fool as you.

DAMIS

What! shall I suffer a censorious bigot to usurp an absolute authority in the family? And shall not we take the least diversion, if this precious spark thinks not fit to allow of it?

DORINE

If one were to hearken to him, and give in to his maxims, we could do nothing but what would be made a crime of; for the critical zealot controls everything.

Mme PERNELLE

And whatever he controls is well controlled. He would fain show you the way to Heaven; and my son ought to make you all love him.

DAMIS

No, look you, madame, neither father nor anything else can oblige me to have any regard for him. I should belie my heart to tell you otherwise. To me his actions are perfectly odious; and I foresee that, one time or other, matters will come to extremity between that wretch and me.

DORINE

'Tis downright scandalous to see an upstart take on him at that rate here. A vagabond that had not a pair of shoes to his feet when he came hither, and all the clothes on his back would not fetch sixpence, that he should so far forget himself as to contradict everything and to play the master.

Mme PERNELLE

Mercy on me! Matters would go much better, were everything managed by his pious directions.

DORINE

He passes for a saint in your imagination; but, believe me, all he does is nothing but hypocrisy.

Mme PERNELLE
What a tongue!

DORINE
I would not trust him without good security, any more than I would his man Laurence.

Mme PERNELLE
What the servant may be at bottom, I can't tell; but I'll answer for the master that he is a good man; you wish him ill, and reject him, only because he tells you the naked truth. 'Tis sin that his heart can't brook, and the interest of Heaven is his only motive.

DORINE
Ay; but why, for some time past, can't he endure that anybody should come near us? How can a civil visit offend Heaven, so much that we must have a

din about it, enough to stun one? Among friends, shall I give you my opinion of the matter?

pointing to Elmire

I take him, in troth, to be jealous of my lady.

Mme PERNELLE

Hold your peace, and consider what you say. He is not the only person who condemns these visits. The bustle that attends the people you keep company with, these coaches continually planted at the gate, and the noisy company of such a parcel of footmen disturb the whole neighbourhood. I am willing to believe there's no harm done; but then it gives people occasion to talk, and that is not well.

CLÉANTE

Alas, madame, will you hinder people from prating? It would be a very hard thing in life, if for any foolish stories that might be raised about people, they should be forced to renounce their best friends; and suppose we should resolve to do so, do you think it would keep all the world from talking? There's no guarding against calumny. Let us therefore not mind silly tittle-tattle, and let's endeavour to live innocently ourselves, and leave the gossiping part of mankind to say what they please.

DORINE

May not neighbour Daphne and her little spouse be the persons who speak ill of us? People whose own conduct is the most ridiculous are always readiest to detract from that of others. They never fail readily to catch at the slightest appearance of an affair, to set the news about with joy, and to give things the very turn they would have them take. By colouring other people's actions like their own, they think to justify their conduct to the world, and fondly hope, by way of some resemblance, to give their own intrigues the air of innocence or to shift part of the blame elsewhere, which they find falls too hard upon themselves.

Mme PERNELLE

All these arguments are nothing to the purpose. Orante is known to lead an exemplary life, her care is all for Heaven; and I have heard say that she has but an indifferent opinion of the company that frequents your house.

DORINE

An admirable pattern indeed! She's a mighty good lady, and lives strictly, 'tis true, but 'tis age that has brought this ardent zeal upon her; and we know that she's a prude in her own defence. As long as 'twas in her power to make conquests, she did not balk any of her advantages; but when she found the lustre of her eyes abate, she would needs renounce the world that was on

7

the point of leaving her; and under the specious mask of great prudence, conceals the decay of her worn-out charms. That is the antiquated coquettes' last shift. It is hard upon them to see themselves deserted by all their gallants. Thus forsaken, their gloomy disquiet can find no relief but in prudery; and then the severity of these good ladies censures all and forgives none. They cry out aloud upon every one's way of living, not out of a principle of charity, but envy, as not being able to suffer that another should taste those pleasures which people on the decline have no relish for.

to Elmire

Mme PERNELLE

These are the idle stories that are told to please you, daughter. There's no getting in a word at your house, for madame here engrosses all the talk to herself. But I shall also be heard in my turn. I tell you my son never acted a wiser part than when he took this devout man into his family; that Heaven in time of need sent him hither to reclaim your wandering minds; that 'tis your main interest to hearken to his counsels, and that he reproves nothing that is not blameable. These visits, balls, and assemblies are all the inventions of the wicked spirit; there's not one word of godliness to be heard at any of them, but idle stuff, nonsense, and tales of a tub, and the neighbours often come in for a share; there's nobody they'll stop at to vilify. In short, the heads of reasonable people are turned by the confusion of such meetings. A thousand different fancies are started about less than nothing; and as a good doctor said the other day very well, 'Tis a perfect Tower of Babel, for every one here babbles out of all measure. Now to give you an account of where all this comes in. . . .

pointing to Cléante

What! is that spark giggling already? Go look for your fool to make a jest of, and unless—

to Elmire

Good-bye t'ye, daughter, I shall say no more. Depend on it, I have not half the esteem for your house I had, and it shall be very fine weather when I set my foot in your doors again.

giving Flipote a box on the ear

Come, you, you're dreaming and gaping at the crows; i'fakins! I'll warm your ears for you. Let's march, trollop, let's march.

exeunt all except Cléante and Dorine

CLÉANTE

I won't go, for fear she should fall foul on me again. That this good old lady—

DORINE

'Tis pity, truly, she does not hear you call her so; she'd give you to understand how she liked you, and that she was not old enough to be called so yet.

CLÉANTE

What a heat has she been in with us about nothing! And how fond does she seem of her Tartuffe!

DORINE

Oh! truly, all this is nothing compared to the infatuation of her son, and were you to see him you'd say he was much worse. His behaviour in our public troubles had procured him the character of a man of sense, and of bravery for his prince; but he's grown quite besotted since he became fond of Tartuffe. He calls him brother, and loves him in his heart a hundred times better than either mother, son, daughter, or wife. He's the only confidant of all his secrets, and the wise director of all his actions; he caresses, he embraces him, and I think one could not have more affection for a mistress. He will have him seated at the upper end of the table, and is delighted to see him gobble as much as half a dozen. He must be helped to all the tit-bits, and whenever he but belches, he bids G—d bless him. In short, he dotes upon him, he's his all, his hero; he admires all he does, quotes him on all occasions, looks on every trifling action of his as a wonder, and every word an oracle. At the same time the fellow, knowing his blind side and willing to make the most on't, has a hundred tricks to impose upon his judgment and get his money from him in the way of bigotry. He now pretends truly to take the whole family to task; even the awkward fool his foot-boy takes upon him to lecture us with his fanatic face, and to demolish our patches, paint, and ribbons. The rascal, the other day, tore us a fine handkerchief that lay in the *Pilgrim's Progress,* and cried that it was a horrid profanation to mix hellish ornaments with sanctified things.

enter Elmire, Mariane, Damis

ELMIRE

to Cléante

You are very happy in not having come to the harangue she gave us at the gate. But I saw my husband, and as he did not see me, I'll go up to wait his coming.

CLÉANTE

I'll wait for him here by way of a little amusement, only bid him good-morrow.

exeunt Elmire and Mariane

9

DAMIS

Hint something to him about my sister's wedding; I suspect that Tartuffe's against it, and that he puts my father upon these tedious evasions; you are not ignorant how nearly I am concerned in it. If my friend Valère and my sister are sincerely fond of one another, his sister, you know, is no less dear to me, and if it must—

DORINE

Here he is.

exit Damis
enter Orgon

ORGON

Hah! brother, good-morrow.

CLÉANTE

I was just going, and am glad to see you come back. The country at present is not very pleasant.

ORGON

Dorine.

to Cléante

Brother, pray stay; you'll give me leave just to inquire the news of the family; I can't be easy else.

to Dorine

Have matters gone well the two days I have been away? What has happened here? How do they all do?

DORINE

My lady the day before yesterday had a fever all day, and was sadly out of order with a strange headache.

ORGON

And Tartuffe?

DORINE

Tartuffe? Extremely well, fat, fair, and fresh-coloured.

ORGON

Poor man!

DORINE

At night she had no stomach, and could not touch a bit of supper, the pain in her head continued so violent.

ORGON

And Tartuffe?

DORINE

He supped by himself before her, and very heartily ate a brace of partridge, and half a leg of mutton hashed.

ORGON

Poor man!

DORINE

She never closed her eyes, but burnt so that she could not get a wink of sleep; and we were forced to sit up with her all night.

ORGON

And Tartuffe?

DORINE

Being agreeably sleepy, he went from table to his chamber, and so into a warm bed, and slept comfortably till next morning.

ORGON

The poor man!

DORINE

At length my lady, prevailed upon by our persuasions, resolved to be let blood; then she soon grew easier.

ORGON

And Tartuffe?

DORINE

He plucked up his spirit, as he should; and fortifying his mind against all evils, to make amends for the blood my lady lost, drank at breakfast four swingeing draughts of wine.

ORGON

The poor man!

DORINE

At present they both are pretty well, and I shall go before and let my lady know how glad you are of her recovery.

exit Dorine

CLÉANTE

She jokes upon you, brother, to your face; and without any design of making you angry, I must tell you freely that 'tis not without reason. Was ever such a whim heard of? Is it possible that a man can be so bewitching at this time of day as to make you forget everything for him? That after having, in your own house, relieved his indigence, you should be ready to—

ORGON

Hold there, brother, you don't know the man you speak of.

CLÉANTE

Well, I don't know him, since you will have it so. But then, in order to know what a man he is, —

ORGON

Brother, you would be charmed did you know him, and there would be no end of your raptures. He's a man—that—ah—a man—a man, in short, a man. Who always practises as he directs, enjoys a profound peace, and regards the whole world no more than so much dung. Ay, I am quite another man by his conversation. He teaches me to set my heart upon nothing; he disengages my mind from friendships or relations; and I could see my brother, children, mother, wife, all expire, and not regard it more than this.

12

CLÉANTE

Humane sentiments, brother, I must confess!

ORGON

Ah! had you but seen him as I first met with him, you would have loved him as well as I do. He came every day to church with a composed mien, and kneeled down just against me. He attracted the eyes of the whole congregation by the fervency with which he sent up his prayers to Heaven. He sighed and groaned very heavily, and every moment humbly kissed the earth. And when I was going out, he would advance before and offer me holy water at the door. Understanding by his boy (who copied him in everything) his low condition and who he was, I made him presents; but he always modestly would offer to return me part. 'Tis too much, he'd say, too much by half. I am not worth your pity. And when I refused to take it again, he would go and give it among the poor before my face. At length Heaven moved me to take him home, since which everything here seems to prosper. I see he reproves without distinction; and that even with regard to my wife, he is extremely cautious of my honour. He acquaints me who ogles her, and is six times more jealous of her than I am. But you can hardly imagine how very good he is. He calls every trifle in himself a sin; he's scandalised at the smallest thing imaginable, so far that the other day he told me he had caught a flea as he was at his devotions, and had killed it, he doubted, in rather too much anger.

CLÉANTE

'Sdeath! you must be mad, brother, I fancy; or do you intend to banter me by such stuff? What is it you mean? All this fooling—

ORGON

Brother, what you say savours of libertinism. You are a little tainted with it; and, as I have told you more than once, you'll draw down some heavy judgment on your head one day or other.

CLÉANTE

This is the usual strain of such as you. They would have everybody as blind as themselves. To be clear-sighted is libertinism, and such as don't dote upon empty grimaces have neither faith nor respect to sacred things. Come, come, all this discourse of yours frights not me; I know what I say, and Heaven sees my heart. We are not to be slaves to your men of form. There are pretenders to devotion as well as to courage. And as we never find the truly brave to be such as make much noise wheresoever they are led by honour, so the good and truly pious, who are worthy of our imitation, are never those that deal much in grimace. Pray, would you make no distinction between hypocrisy and true devotion? Would you term them both alike, and pay the same regard to the mask as you do to the face? Would you put artifice on the level with sincerity, and confound appearance with reality? Is the phantom of the same esteem with you as the figure? and is bad money of the same value as good? Men generally are odd creatures. They never keep up to true nature. The bounds of reason are too narrow for them. In every character they overact their parts, and the noblest designs very often suffer in their hands because they will be running things into extremes and always carry things too far. This, brother, by the by.

ORGON

Yes, yes, you are without doubt a very reverend doctor; all the knowledge in the world lies under your cap. You are the only wise and discerning man, the oracle, the Cato of the present age; all men, compared to you, are downright fools.

CLÉANTE

No, brother, I am none of your reverend sages, nor is the whole learning of the universe vested in me; but I must tell you I have wit enough to distinguish truth from falsehood. And as I see no character in life more great or valuable than to be truly devout, nor anything more noble, or more beautiful, than the fervour of a sincere piety, so I think nothing more abominable than the outside daubing of a pretended zeal, than those mountebanks, those devotees in show, whose sacrilegious and treacherous grimace deceives with impunity, and according as they please, make a jest of what is most venerable and sacred among men. Those slaves of interest who make a trade of godliness, and who would purchase honours and reputation with a hypocritical turning up of the eyes and affected transports. Those people, I say, who show an uncommon zeal for the next world in order to make their fortunes in this, who, with great affectation and earnestness, daily recommend solitude, while they live in courts. Men who know how to make their own vices consistent with their zeal; they are passionate, revengeful, faithless, full of artifice; and to effect a man's destruction, they insolently urge their private resentment as the cause of Heaven; being so much the more dangerous in their wrath as they point against us those weapons which men reverence, and because their passions prompt them to assassinate us with a consecrated blade. There are too many of this vile character, but the sincerely devout are easily known; our age, brother, affords us some of these who might serve for glorious patterns to us. Observe Aristo, Periander, Orontes, Alcidamas, Polidore, Clitander; that title is refused to them by nobody. These are not braggadocios in virtue. We see none of this insufferable haughtiness in their conduct, and their devotion is humane and gentle. They censure not all we do, they think there's too much pride in these corrections, and leaving the fierceness of words to others, reprove our actions by their own. They never

build upon the appearance of a fault, and are always ready to judge favour-
ably of others. They have no cabals, no intrigues to carry on; their chief
aim is to live themselves as they should do. They never worry a poor sinner;
their quarrel is only with the offence. Nor do they ever exert a keener zeal
for the interest of Heaven than Heaven itself does. These are the men for me;
this is the true practice, and this the example fit to be followed. Your man is
indeed not of this stamp. You cry up his zeal out of a good intention, but I
believe you are imposed on by a very false gloss.

ORGON

My dear brother, have you done?

CLÉANTE

Yes.

ORGON   *going*

Then I'm your humble servant.

CLÉANTE

Pray one word more, brother; let us leave this discourse. You know you
promised to take Valère for your son-in-law.

ORGON

Yes.

CLÉANTE

And have appointed a day for this agreeable wedding.

ORGON

True.

CLÉANTE

Why then do you put off the solemnity?

ORGON

I can't tell.

CLÉANTE

Have you some other design in your head?

ORGON

Perhaps so.

CLÉANTE

Will you break your word, then?

15

ORGON
I don't say that.

CLÉANTE
I think there's no obstacle can hinder you from performing your promise.

ORGON
That's as it happens.

CLÉANTE
Does the speaking of a single word require so much circumspection, then?
Valère sends me to you about it.

ORGON
Heaven be praised!

CLÉANTE
What answer shall I return him?

ORGON
What you will.

CLÉANTE
But 'tis necessary I should know your intentions; pray what are they?

ORGON
To do just what Heaven pleases.

CLÉANTE
But to the point, pray. Valère has your promise; do you stand to it, ay or no?

ORGON
Good be t'ye.

alone **CLÉANTE**
I am afraid he'll meet with some misfortune in his love. I ought to inform
him how matters go.

ACT II

Orgon, Mariane

ORGON
Mariane!

MARIANE
Sir.

ORGON
Come hither; I have something to say to you in private.

MARIANE

to Orgon, who is looking into a closet

What are you looking for, sir?

ORGON
I'm looking if anybody's there who might overhear us. This little place is fit for such a purpose. So, we're all safe. I have always, Mariane, found you of a sweet disposition, and you have always been very dear to me.

MARIANE

I am very much obliged to you, sir, for your fatherly affection.

ORGON

'Tis very well said, daughter, and to deserve it, your chief care should be to make me easy.

MARIANE

That is the height of my ambition.

ORGON

Very well. Then what say you of Tartuffe, our guest?

MARIANE

Who, I?

ORGON

Yes, you; pray take heed how you answer.

MARIANE

Alas! sir, I'll say what you will of him.

*Dorine
comes in softly,
and stands
behind Orgon
without being seen*

ORGON

That's discreetly said. Tell me then, my girl, that he's a very deserving person, that you like him, and that it would be agreeable if, with my consent, you might have him for a husband, ha?

MARIANE

How, sir?

ORGON

What's the matter?

MARIANE

What said you?

ORGON

What?

MARIANE

Did I mistake you?

ORGON
As how?

MARIANE
Whom would you have me say I liked, sir, and should be glad, with your
approbation, to have for a husband?

ORGON
Tartuffe.

MARIANE
I protest to you, sir, there's nothing in it. Why would you make me tell you
such a story?

ORGON
But I would have it to be no story, and 'tis enough that I have pitched upon
him for you.

MARIANE
What, would you, sir—

ORGON
Ay, child, I purpose, by your marriage, to join Tartuffe to my family. I
have resolved upon't, and as I have a right to—
spying Dorine
What business have you
there? Your curiosity is very great, sweetheart, to bring you to listen in
this manner.

DORINE
In troth, sir, whether this report proceeds from conjecture or chance, I
don't know; but they have been just telling me the news of this match, and
I have been making a very great jest of it.

ORGON
Why, is the thing so incredible?

DORINE
So incredible that were you to tell me so yourself, I should not believe you.

ORGON
I know how to make you believe it, though.

DORINE
Ay, ay, sir, you tell us a comical story.

ORGON

I tell you just what will prove true in a short time.

DORINE

Stuff!

to Mariane

ORGON

Daughter, I promise you I'm not in jest.

DORINE

Go, go; don't believe your father, madame, he does but joke.

ORGON

I tell you—

DORINE

No, 'tis in vain, nobody will believe you.

ORGON

My anger at length—

DORINE

Well, sir, we will believe you; and so much the worse on your side. What, sir, is it possible that with that air of wisdom, and that spacious beard on your face, you should be weak enough but to wish—

ORGON

Harkee, you have taken certain liberties of late that I dislike. I tell you that, child.

DORINE

Good sir, let us argue this affair calmly. You really must banter people by this scheme. Your daughter is not cut out for a bigot; he has other things to think on. And then, what will such an alliance bring you in? For what reason would you go, with all your wealth, to choose a beggar for a son-in-law—

ORGON

Hold your tongue! If he has nothing, know that we ought to esteem him for it. His poverty is an honest poverty which raises him above all grandeur, because he has suffered himself, in short, to be deprived of his fortune by his negligence for things temporal and his strong attachment to things eternal. But my assistance may put him in a way of getting out of trouble and of recovering his own. As poor as he is, he's a gentleman, and the estate he was born to is not inconsiderable.

20

DORINE

Yes, he says so; and this vanity, sir, does not very well suit with piety. He
that embraces the simplicity of a holy life should not set forth his name and
family so much. The humble procedure of devotion does but ill agree with
the glare of ambition. To what purpose all this pride?—But this talk offends you. Then let us lay aside his quality, and speak to his person. Can you
have the heart to fling away such a girl as this upon such a man as he? Should
you not consult propriety, and look a little forward to the consequences of
such a union as this? Depend upon't, a young woman's virtue is in some
danger when she isn't married to her mind; that her living virtuously after-
ward depends, in a great measure, upon the good qualities of her husband;
and that those whom people everywhere point at with the finger to the fore-
head, often make their wives what we find they are. It is no easy task to be
faithful to some sorts of husbands; and he that gives his daughter a man she
hates, is accountable to Heaven for the slips she makes. Consider then to
what danger your design exposes you.

ORGON

I tell you, she is to learn from me what to do.

DORINE

You could not do better with her than to follow my advice.

ORGON

Don't let us amuse ourselves, daughter, with this silly stuff. I am your father, and know what you must do. I had indeed promised you to Valère, but, besides that 'tis reported he is given to play, I suspect him of being a little profligate. I don't observe that he frequents the church.

DORINE

Would you have him run to church at your precise hours, as people do who go there only to be taken notice of?

ORGON

I am not consulting you about it.

to his daughter

The other, in short, is a favourite of Heaven, and that is beyond any other possessions. This union will crown your wishes with every sort of good; it will be one continued scene of pleasure and delight. You'll live in faithful love together, really like two children, like two turtle-doves. No unhappy debate will e'er rise between you; and you'll make anything of him you can well desire.

DORINE

She? She'll ne'er make anything but a fool of him, I assure you.

ORGON

Hey! What language!

DORINE

I say, he has the look of a fool; and his ascendant will overbear all the virtue your daughter has.

ORGON

Have done with your interruptions. Learn to hold your peace, and don't you put in your oar where you have nothing to do.

DORINE

Nay, sir, I only speak for your good.

ORGON

You are too officious. Pray hold your tongue, if you please.

22

DORINE

If one had not a love for you—

ORGON

I desire none of your love.

DORINE

But I will love you, sir, in spite of your teeth.

ORGON

Ha!

DORINE

I have your reputation much at heart, and can't bear to have you made the subject of every gossip's tale.

ORGON

Then you won't have done?

DORINE

It would be a sin to let you make such an alliance as this.

ORGON

Will you hold your tongue, you serpent, whose impudence—

DORINE

Oh! what, a devotee, and fly into such a rage?

ORGON

Yes, my choler is moved at this impertinence, and I'm resolved you shall hold your tongue.

DORINE

Be it so. But though I don't speak a word, I don't think the less.

ORGON

Think if you will, but take care not to say a syllable to me about it, or— Enough—

to his daughter

I have maturely weighed all things as a wise man should.

DORINE   *aside*

It makes me mad that I must not speak now!

ORGON

Tartuffe, without foppery, is a person so formed—

DORINE

aside

Yes, 'tis a pretty phiz.

ORGON

That should you have no great relish for his other qualifications—

DORINE

aside

She'll have a very fine bargain of him!

Orgon turns about towards Dorine, and eyes her with his arms across.

Were I in her place, though, no man alive should marry me against my will, with impunity. I'd let him see, soon after the ceremony was over, that a wife has a revenge always at hand.

ORGON

to Dorine

Then what I say, stands for nothing with you?

DORINE

What do you complain of? I don't speak to you.

ORGON

What is it you do then?

DORINE

I talk to myself.

ORGON

aside

Very well! I must give her a slap on the face, to correct her prodigious insolence.

He puts himself into a posture to strike Dorine, and at every word he speaks to his daughter he casts his eyes upon Dorine, who stands bolt-upright, without speaking.

Daughter, you must needs approve of my design—and believe that the husband—which I have picked out for you—

to Dorine

Why dost thou not talk to thyself now?

DORINE

Because I have nothing to say to myself.

ORGON

One little word more.

DORINE
I've no mind to it.

ORGON
To be sure I watched you.

DORINE
A downright fool, i'faith.

ORGON *to Mariane*

In short, daughter, you must obey, and show an entire deference for my choice.

DORINE *as she runs off*
I should scorn to take such a husband myself.

ORGON *strikes at her, but misses*

You have a pestilent hussy with you there, daughter, that I can't live with any longer, without sin. I'm not in a condition to proceed at present; her insolence has put my spirits into such a ferment that I must go take the air to recover myself a little.

*exit Orgon
enter Dorine*

DORINE

Pray tell me, have you lost your tongue? Must I play your part for you on this occasion? What, suffer a silly overture to be made you, without saying the least word against it!

MARIANE
What should one do with a positive father?

DORINE
Anything, to ward off such a menace.

MARIANE
But what?

DORINE

Why, tell him that hearts admit of no proxies; that you marry for yourself, and not for him; that you being the person for whom the whole affair is transacted, your inclinations for the man should be consulted, not his; and that if Tartuffe seems so lovely in his eyes, he may marry him himself without let or hindrance.

MARIANE

A father, I own, has such a command over one that I never had courage to make him a reply.

DORINE

But let us reason the case. Valère has made advances for you; pray, do you love him, or do you not?

MARIANE

Nay, you do injustice to my love, to question my affections! Ought you, Dorine, to ask me that? Have I not opened my heart to you a hundred times on that subject? and are you still a stranger to the warmth of my passion?

DORINE

How do I know whether your heart and words keep pace together? or whether you really have any particular regard for this lover or not?

MARIANE

You do me wrong, Dorine, to doubt it; and the sincerity of my sentiments, in that matter, has been but too plain.

DORINE

You really love him, then?

MARIANE

Ay, extremely.

DORINE

And according to all appearance, he loves you as well.

MARIANE

I believe so.

DORINE

And you two have a mutual desire to marry?

MARIANE

Assuredly.

DORINE

What is then your expectation from this other match?

MARIANE

To kill myself, if they force me to it.

DORINE

Very good! That's a relief I did not think of; you need only to die to get rid of this perplexity. 'Tis a wonderful remedy, for certain. It makes one mad to hear folks talk at this rate.

MARIANE

Bless me, Dorine! what a humour are you got into! You have no compassion upon people's afflictions.

DORINE

I have no compassion for people who talk idly and give way in time of action as you do.

MARIANE

But what would you have, if one is timorous?

DORINE

But love requires a firmness of mind.

MARIANE

But have I wavered in my affections towards Valère? And is it not his business to gain me of my father?

DORINE

But what? if your father be a downright humorist, who is entirely bewitched with his Tartuffe, and would set aside a match he had agreed on, pray is that your lover's fault?

MARIANE

But should I, by a flat and confident refusal, let everybody know that I am violently in love? Would you have me, for his sake, transgress the modesty of my sex and the bounds of my duty? Would you have my passion become a perfect town-talk?

DORINE

No, no, I don't want anything. I see you'd fain have Monsieur Tartuffe; and now I think of it, I should be in the wrong to dissuade you from so considerable an alliance. To what purpose should I oppose your inclinations? The match is in itself too advantageous. Monsieur Tartuffe, oh! is this a trifling offer? If we take it right, he's no simpleton. It will be no small honour to be his mate. All the world has a prodigious value for him already; he is well born, handsome in his person, he has a red ear, and a very florid complexion; you'll, in short, be but too happy with such a husband.

MARIANE
Heavens!

DORINE
You can't conceive what a joy 'twill be to you to be the consort of so fine a man!

MARIANE
Poh! prithee give over this discourse, and rather assist me against this match. 'Tis now all over; I yield, and am ready to do whatever you'd have me.

DORINE
No, no, a daughter should do as she's bid, though her father would have her marry a monkey. Besides, what reason have you to complain? Yours is a benefit ticket. You'll be coached down to his own borough-town, which you'll find abounds in cousins and uncles. It will be very diverting to you to entertain them all. Then Madame Tartuffe will be directly introduced to the beau-monde. You'll go visit, by way of welcome, the bailiff's lady and the assessor's wife; they'll do you the honour of the folding chair. At a good time you may hope for a ball, and a great consort, to wit, two pair of bag-pipes; and perchance you may see merry-Andrew and the puppet-show; if, however, your husband—

MARIANE
Oh! you kill me! Rather contrive how to help me by your advice.

DORINE
Your humble servant for that.

MARIANE
Nay, Dorine, for Heaven's sake—

DORINE
No, it must be a match, to punish you.

MARIANE
Dear girl, do!

DORINE
No.

MARIANE
If my professions—

DORINE

No, Tartuffe's your man, and you shall have a taste of him.

MARIANE

You know how much I always confided in you; be so good—

DORINE

No, in troth; you shall be Tartuffed.

MARIANE

Well, since my misfortunes can't move you, henceforth leave me entirely to my despair. That shall lend my heart relief, and I known an infallible remedy for all my sufferings.

offers to go

DORINE

Here, here, come back; I'm appeased. I must take compassion on you, for all this.

MARIANE

I tell you, d'y' see, Dorine, if they do expose me to this torment, it will certainly cost me my life.

DORINE

Don't vex yourself, it may easily be prevented—But see, here's your humble servant Valère.

enter Valère

VALÈRE

I was just now told an odd piece of news, madame, that I knew nothing of, and which to be sure is very pretty.

MARIANE

What's that?

VALÈRE

That you are to be married to Tartuffe.

MARIANE

'Tis certain my father has such a design in his head.

VALÈRE

Your father, madame—

MARIANE

Has altered his mind, and has been just now making the proposal to me.

29

VALÈRE
What, seriously?

MARIANE
Ay, seriously. He has been declaring himself strenuously for the match.

VALÈRE
And pray, madame, what may be your determination in the affair?

MARIANE
I don't know.

VALÈRE
The answer is honest! You don't know?

MARIANE
No.

VALÈRE
No?

MARIANE
What would you advise me to?

VALÈRE
I advise you to accept of him for a husband.

MARIANE
Is that your advice?

VALÈRE
Yes.

MARIANE
In good earnest?

VALÈRE
No doubt of it. The choice is good, and well worth attending to.

MARIANE
Well, sir, I shall take your counsel.

VALÈRE
You will have no difficulty to follow it, I believe.

MARIANE

Hardly more than your counsel gave you.

VALÈRE

I gave it, madame, to please you.

MARIANE

And I shall follow it, to do you a pleasure.

DORINE

So. Let's see what this will come to.

retiring to the farther part of the stage

VALÈRE

Is this, then, your affection? And was it all deceit, when you—

MARIANE

Pray let's talk no more of that. You told me frankly that I ought to accept of the offer made me. And I tell you, I shall do so, only because you advise me to it as the best.

VALÈRE

Don't excuse yourself upon my intentions. Your resolution was made before, and you now lay hold of a frivolous pretence for the breaking of your word.

MARIANE

'Tis true; it's well said.

VALÈRE

Doubtless, and you never had any true love for me.

MARIANE

Alas! You may think so if you please.

VALÈRE

Yes, yes, may think so; but my offended heart may chance to be beforehand with you in that affair, and I can tell where to offer both my addresses and my hand.

MARIANE

I don't doubt it, sir. The warmth that merit raises—

VALÈRE

Lack-a-day! Let us drop merit. I have little enough of that, and you think

31

so; but I hope another will treat me in a kinder manner; and I know a person whose heart, open to my retreat, will not be ashamed to make up my loss.

MARIANE
The loss is not great, and you will be comforted upon this change easily enough.

VALÈRE
You may believe I shall do all that lies in my power. A heart that forgets us, engages our glory; we must employ our utmost cares to forget it too; and if we don't succeed, we must at least pretend we do; for to show a regard for those that forsake us, is a meanness one cannot answer to one's self.

MARIANE
The sentiment is certainly noble and sublime.

VALÈRE
Very well, and what everybody must approve of. What? would you have me languish for ever for you? See you fly into another's arms before my face, and not transfer my slighted affections somewhere else?

MARIANE

So far from that, 'tis what I would have; and I wish 'twere done already.

VALÈRE

You wish it done?

MARIANE

Yes.

VALÈRE

That's insulting me sufficiently, madame; I am just going to give you that satisfaction.

he offers to go

MARIANE

'Tis very well.

VALÈRE

returning

Be pleased to remember, at least, that 'tis yourself who drive me to this extremity.

MARIANE

Yes.

VALÈRE

returning again

And that the design I have conceived is only from your example.

MARIANE

My example be it.

VALÈRE

going

Enough, you shall soon be punctually obeyed.

MARIANE

So much the better.

VALÈRE

returning again

'Tis the last time I shall ever trouble you.

MARIANE

With all my heart.

33

goes toward the door and returns

VALÈRE

Hey?

MARIANE

What's the matter?

VALÈRE

Didn't you call me?

MARIANE

Who, I? You dream, sure.

VALÈRE

Well, then, I'll be gone; farewell, madame!

MARIANE

Fare ye well, sir.

to Mariane

DORINE

I think, for my part, by this piece of extravagance, you've both lost your senses. I have let you alone thus long squabbling, to see what end you'd make of it. Hark ye, Monsieur Valère!

she lays hold of Valère's arm

pretending to resist

VALÈRE

Hey! What would you have, Dorine?

DORINE

Come hither.

VALÈRE

No, no, my indignation overpowers me; don't hinder me from doing as she would have me.

DORINE

Stay.

VALÈRE

No, d'ye see, I'm resolved upon it.

DORINE

Ah!

MARIANE *aside*

He's uneasy at the sight of me. My presence drives him away; I had much better therefore leave the place.

DORINE *quitting Valère, and running after Mariane*

What, t'other? whither do you run?

MARIANE

Let me alone.

DORINE

You must come back.

MARIANE

No, no, Dorine; in vain you'd hold me.

VALÈRE *aside*

I find that my presence is but a plague to her. I had certainly better free her from it.

DORINE *quitting Mariane, and running after Valère*

What, again? Deuce take you for me. Leave this fooling, and come hither both of you.

she takes Valère and Mariane by the hand, and brings them back

VALÈRE

But what's your design?

MARIANE

What would you do?

DORINE

Set you two to rights again, and bring you out of this scrape.

to Valère

Aren't you mad, to wrangle at this rate?

VALÈRE

Didn't you hear how she spoke to me?

35

DORINE

to Mariane

Weren't you a simpleton, to be in such a passion?

MARIANE

Didn't you see the thing, and how he treated me?

DORINE

Folly on both sides.

to Valère

She has nothing more at heart than that she may be one day yours; I am witness to it.

to Mariane

He loves none but yourself, and has no other ambition than to become your husband, I answer for it upon my life.

MARIANE

to Valère

Why then did you give me such advice?

VALÈRE

to Mariane

And why was I consulted upon such a subject?

DORINE

You're a couple of fools. Come, come, your hands, both of you;

to Valère

come, you.

VALÈRE

giving his hand to Dorine

What will my hand do?

DORINE

to Mariane

So; come, now yours.

MARIANE

giving her hand

To what purpose is all this?

DORINE

Come along, come quick: you love one another better than you think of.

VALÈRE

turning toward Mariane

But don't do things with an ill grace, and give a body a civil look.

36

Mariane turns toward Valère, and smiles a little

DORINE

In troth, lovers are silly creatures!

VALÈRE

to Mariane

Now, have I not room to complain of you; and, without lying, were not you a wicked creature, to gratify yourself in saying a thing so very shocking to me?

MARIANE

But are not you the ungratefullest man in the world—

DORINE

Come let's adjourn this debate till another time; and think how to ward off this plaguy wedding.

MARIANE

Say, then, what engines shall we set at work?

DORINE

We'll set them every way to work.

to Mariane

Your father's in jest;

to Valère

it must be nothing but talk.

to Mariane

But for your part, your best way will be to carry the appearance of a gentle compliance with his extravagance, that so, in case of an alarm, you may have it more easily in your power to delay the marriage proposed. In gaining time we shall remedy everything. Sometimes you may fob 'em off with some illness, which is to come all of a sudden and will require delay. Sometimes you may fob 'em off with ill omens. You unluckily met a corpse, broke a looking-glass, or dreamed dirty water; and at last, the best on't is, they can't possibly join you to any other but him, unless you please to say, Yes. But, the better to carry on the design, I think it proper you should not be seen conferring together.

to Valère

Go you immediately and employ your friends, that he may be forced to keep his word with you.

to Mariane

Let us go excite his brother's endeavours, and engage the mother-in-law in our party. Adieu.

VALÈRE

to Mariane

Whatever efforts any of us may be preparing, my greatest hope, to say the truth, is in you.

MARIANE

to Valère

I can't promise for the inclinations of a father, but I shall be none but Valère's.

VALÈRE

How you transport me! And though I durst—

DORINE

Ah! These lovers are never weary of prattling. Away, I tell you.

VALÈRE

goes a step or two, and returns

Once more—

DORINE

What a clack is yours! Draw you off this way, and you t'other.

pushing them each out by the shoulders

ACT III

Damis, Dorine

DAMIS

May thunder, this moment, strike me dead; let me be everywhere treated like the greatest scoundrel alive, if any respect or power whatever shall stop me, and if I don't strike some masterly stroke.

DORINE

Moderate your passion for Heaven's sake; your father did but barely mention it. People don't do all they propose, and the distance is great from the project to the execution.

DAMIS

I must put a stop to this fool's projects, and tell him a word or two in his ear.

DORINE

Gently, gently, pray; let your mother-in-law alone with him, as well as with your father. She has some credit with Tartuffe. He is mighty complaisant to all she says, and perhaps he may have a sneaking kindness for her. I would to Heaven it were true! That would be charming. In short, your interest obliges her to send for him; she has a mind to sound his intentions with regard to the wedding that disturbs you, and represent to him the fatal feuds he will raise in the family if he entertains any hopes of this affair. His man says that he's at prayers, and I could not see him. But this servant told me he would not be long before he came down. Then pray be gone, and let me stay for him.

DAMIS

I may be present at this whole conference.

DORINE

No, they must be by themselves.

DAMIS

I shall say nothing to him.

DORINE

You're mistaken; we know the usual impatience of your temper, and 'tis the ready way to spoil all. Get away.

DAMIS

No, I will see him without putting myself in a passion.

DORINE

How troublesome you are! He's coming; retire.

Damis conceals himself in a closet enter Tartuffe

TARTUFFE

upon seeing Dorine speaks aloud to his servant who is in the house

Laurence, lock up my hair-cloth and scourge, and beg of Heaven ever to enlighten you with grace. If anybody comes to see me, I am gone to the prisons to distribute my alms.

DORINE

aside

What affectation and roguery!

TARTUFFE
What do you want?

40

DORINE

To tell you —

TARTUFFE

drawing a handkerchief out of his pocket

Oh! lack-a-day! pray take me this handkerchief before you speak.

DORINE

What for?

TARTUFFE

Cover that bosom, which I can't bear to see. Such objects hurt the soul, and usher in sinful thoughts.

DORINE

You mightily melt then at a temptation, and the flesh makes great impression upon your senses? Truly, I can't tell what heat may inflame you; but, for my part, I am not so apt to hanker. Now I could see you stark naked from head to foot, and that whole hide of yours not tempt me at all.

TARTUFFE

Pray, now, speak with a little modesty, or I shall leave you this minute.

DORINE

No, no, 'tis I who am going to leave you to yourself; and I have only two words to say to you: My lady is coming down into this parlour, and desires the favour of a word with you.

TARTUFFE

Alack! with all my heart.

aside

DORINE

How sweet he grows upon it! I'faith, I still stand to what I said of him.

TARTUFFE

Will she come presently?

DORINE

I think I hear her. Ay, 'tis she herself; I leave you together.

exit Dorine
enter Elmire

TARTUFFE

May Heaven, of its goodness, ever bestow upon you health both of body and of mind! and bless your days equal to the wish of the lowest of its votaries!

ELMIRE

I am much obliged to you for this pious wish; but let us take a seat to be more at ease.

sitting down

TARTUFFE

Do you find your indisposition anything abated?

sitting

ELMIRE

Very well; my fever soon left me.

TARTUFFE

My prayers have not sufficient merit to have drawn down this favour from above, but I made no vows to Heaven that did not concern your recovery.

ELMIRE

Your zeal for me was too solicitous.

42

TARTUFFE

Your dear health cannot be overrated; and, to re-establish it, I could have sacrificed my own.

ELMIRE

That is carrying Christian charity a great way, and I am highly indebted to you for all this goodness.

TARTUFFE

I do much less for you than you deserve.

ELMIRE

I had a desire to speak with you in private on a certain affair, and am glad that nobody observes us here.

TARTUFFE

I am also overjoyed at it; and, be sure, it can be no ordinary satisfaction, madame, to find myself alone with you. 'Tis an opportunity that I have hitherto petitioned Heaven for in vain.

ELMIRE

What I want to talk with you upon is a small matter in which your whole heart must be open and hide nothing from me.

TARTUFFE

And, for this singular favour, I certainly will unbosom myself to you without the least reserve; and I protest to you that the stir I made about the visits paid here to your charms, was not out of hatred to you, but rather out of a passionate zeal which induced me to it, and out of a pure motive—

ELMIRE

For my part I take it very well, and believe 'tis my good that gives you this concern.

TARTUFFE

taking Elmire's hand, and squeezing her fingers

Yes, madame, without doubt, and such is the fervour of my—

ELMIRE

Oh! you squeeze me too hard.

TARTUFFE

'Tis out of excess of zeal; I never intended to hurt you. I had much rather—

puts his hand upon her knee

43

ELMIRE

What does your hand do there?

TARTUFFE

I'm only feeling your clothes, madame; the stuff is mighty rich.

ELMIRE

Oh! Pray give over; I am very ticklish.

she draws away her chair, and Tartuffe follows with his

TARTUFFE

Bless me! How wonderful is the workmanship of this lace! They work to a miracle nowadays. Things of all kinds were never better done.

ELMIRE

'Tis true; but let us speak to our affair a little. They say that my husband has a mind to set aside his promise, and to give you his daughter. Is that true? Pray tell me.

44

TARTUFFE

He did hint something towards it. But, madame, to tell you the truth, that is not the happiness I sigh after. I behold elsewhere the wonderful attractions of the felicity that engages every wish of mine.

ELMIRE

That is, you love no earthly things.

TARTUFFE

My breast does not enclose a heart of flint.

ELMIRE

I am apt to think that your sighs tend all to Heaven, and that nothing here below can detain your desires.

TARTUFFE

The love which engages us to eternal beauties does not extinguish in us the love of temporal ones. Our senses may easily be charmed with the perfect works Heaven has formed. Its reflected charms shine forth in such as you. But in your person it displays its choicest wonders. It has diffused such beauties o'er your face as surprise the sight and transport the heart; nor could I behold you, perfect creature, without admiring in you the Author of nature, and feeling my heart touched with an ardent love at sight of the fairest of portraits wherein he has delineated himself. At first I was under apprehensions lest this secret flame might be a dexterous surprise of the foul fiend; and my heart even resolved to avoid your eyes, believing you an obstacle to my future happiness. But at length I perceived, most lovely beauty, that my passion could not be blameable, that I could reconcile it with modesty, and this made me abandon my heart to it. It is, I confess, a very great presumption in me to make you the offer of this heart; but, in my vows, I rely wholly on your goodness, and not on anything in my own weak power. In you centre my hope, my happiness, my quiet; on you depend my torment or my bliss; and I am on the point of being, by your sole decision, happy if you will, or miserable if you please.

ELMIRE

The declaration is extremely gallant, but, to say the truth, it is a good deal surprising. Methinks you ought to have fortified your mind better, and to have reasoned a little upon a design of this nature. A devotee as you are, whom every one speaks of as—

TARTUFFE

Ah! being a devotee does not make me the less a man; and when one comes

45

to view your celestial charms, the heart surrenders, and reasons no more. I know that such language from me seems somewhat strange; but, madame, after all, I am not an angel, and should you condemn the declaration I make, you must lay the blame upon your attractive charms. From the moment I first set eyes upon your more than human splendour, you became the sovereign of my soul. The ineffable sweetness of your divine looks broke through the resistance which my heart obstinately made. It surmounted everything, fastings, prayers, tears, and turned all my vows on the side of your charms. My eyes and my sighs have told it you a thousand times, and the better to explain myself I here make use of words. Now if you contemplate with some benignity of soul the tribulations of your unworthy slave; if your goodness will give me consolation, and deign to debase itself so low as my nothingness, I shall ever entertain for you, miracle of sweetness, a devotion which nothing can equal. Your honour, with me, runs no risk, it need fear no disgrace on my part. All those courtly gallants the ladies are so fond of, make a bustle in what they do, and are vain in what they say. We see they are ever vaunting of their success; they receive no favours that they don't divulge, and their indiscreet tongues, which people confide in, dishonour the altar on which their hearts offer sacrifice. But men of our sort burn with a discreet flame, with whom a secret is always sure to remain such. The care we take of our own reputation is an undeniable security to the persons beloved. And 'tis with us, when they accept our hearts, that they enjoy love without scandal and pleasure without fear.

ELMIRE

I hear what you say, and your rhetoric explains itself to me in terms sufficiently strong. Don't you apprehend that I may take a fancy now to acquaint my husband with this gallantry of yours? and that an early account of an amour of this sort might pretty much alter his present affections towards you?

TARTUFFE

I know that you are too good, and that you will rather pardon my temerity; that you will excuse me, upon the score of human frailty, the sallies of a passion that offends you; and will consider, when you consult your glass, that a man is not blind, and is made of flesh and blood.

ELMIRE

Some might take it perhaps in another manner; but I shall show my discretion, and not tell my husband of it. But in return I will have one thing of you, that is honestly and sincerely to forward the match between Valère and Mariane, and that you yourself renounce the unjust power whereby you hope to be enriched with what belongs to another. And—

DAMIS

coming out of the closet where he was hidden

No, madame, no, this ought to be made public. I was in this place and over-heard it all; and the goodness of Heaven seems to have directed me thither to confound the pride of a traitor that wrongs me, to open me a way to take vengeance of his hypocrisy and insolence, to undeceive my father and show him, in a clear light, the soul of a villain that talks to you of love.

ELMIRE

No, Damis, 'tis enough that he reforms and endeavours to deserve the favour I do him. Since I have promised him, don't make me break my word. 'Tis not my humour to make a noise; a wife will make herself merry with such follies and never trouble her husband's ears with them.

DAMIS

You have your reasons for using him in that manner, and I have mine too for acting otherwise. To spare him would be ridiculous; the insolent pride of his bigotry has triumphed too much over my just resentment, and created too many disorders among us already. The rascal has but too long governed my father and opposed my passion, as well as Valère's. 'Tis fit the perfidious wretch should be laid open to him, and Heaven for this purpose offers me an easy way to do it. I am greatly indebted to it for the opportunity; it is too favourable a one to be neglected, and I should deserve to have it taken from me now I have it, should I not make use of it.

ELMIRE

Damis—

DAMIS

No, by your leave, I must take my own counsel. My heart overflows with joy, and all you can say would in vain dissuade me from the pleasure of avenging myself. Without going any farther, I will make an end of the affair, and here's just what will give me satisfaction.

enter Orgon

We are going to entertain you, sir, with an adventure spick and span new, which will very much surprise you. You are well rewarded for all your caresses, and this gentleman makes a fine acknowledgment of your tender-ness. His great zeal for you is just come to light; it aims at nothing less than the dishonour of your bed, and I took him here making an injurious declara-tion of a criminal love to your wife. She is good-natured, and her over-great discretion, by all means, would have kept the secret; but I can't encourage such impudence, and think that not to apprise you of it is to do you an injury.

47

ELMIRE

Yes, I am of opinion that one ought never to break in upon a husband's rest with such idle stuff, that our honour can by no means depend upon it, and that 'tis enough we know how to defend ourselves. These are my thoughts of the matter; and you would have said nothing, Damis, if I had had any credit with you.

exit Elmire

ORGON

Heavens! What have I heard? Is this credible?

TARTUFFE

Yes, brother, I am a wicked, guilty, wretched sinner, full of iniquity, the greatest villain that ever breathed. Every instant of my life is crowded with stains; 'tis one continued series of crimes and defilements; and I see that Heaven, for my punishment, designs to mortify me on this occasion. Whatever great offence they can lay to my charge, I shall have more humility than to deny it. Believe what they tell you, arm your resentment, and like a criminal, drive me out of your house. I cannot have so great a share of shame but I have still deserved a much larger.

to his son

ORGON

Ah, traitor! darest thou, by this falsehood, attempt to tarnish the purity of his virtue?

DAMIS

What! shall the feigned meekness of this hypocritical soul make you give the lie—

ORGON

Thou cursed plague! hold thy tongue.

TARTUFFE

Ah! let him speak; you chide him wrongfully; you had much better believe what he tells you. Why so favourable to me upon such a fact? Do you know after all what I may be capable of? Can you, my brother, depend upon my outside? Do you think me the better for what you see of me? No, no, you suffer yourself to be deceived by appearances, and I am neither better nor worse, alas! than these people think me. The world indeed takes me for a very good man, but the truth is, I am a very worthless creature.

turning to Damis

Yes, my dear

child, say on, call me treacherous, infamous, reprobate, thief, and murderer; load me with names still more detestable; I don't gainsay you; I have deserved them all, and am willing on my knees to suffer the ignominy, as a shame due to the enormities of my life.

ORGON *to Tartuffe*

This is too much, brother.

to his son

Does not thy heart relent, traitor?

DAMIS

What, shall his words so far deceive you as to—

ORGON

Hold your tongue, rascal!

raising Tartuffe

For Heaven's sake, brother, rise.

to his son

Infamous wretch!

DAMIS

He can—

ORGON

Hold thy tongue.

DAMIS

Intolerable! What! am I taken for—

ORGON

Say one other word and I'll break thy bones.

TARTUFFE

For Heaven's sake, brother, don't be angry; I had rather suffer any hardship than that he should get the slightest hurt on my account.

ORGON *to his son*

Ungrateful monster!

TARTUFFE

Let him alone; if I must on my knees ask forgiveness for him—

49

ORGON

throwing himself also at Tartuffe's feet, and embracing him

Alas! You are in jest, sure?

to his son

See his goodness, sirrah!

DAMIS

Then—

ORGON

Have done.

DAMIS

What! I—

ORGON

Peace, I say. I know what put you upon this attack well enough; ye all hate him, and I now see wife, children, servants, are all let loose against him. They impudently try every way to remove this devout person from me. But the more they strive to get him out, the greater care will I take to keep him in; and therefore will I hasten his marriage with my daughter, to confound the pride of the whole family.

DAMIS

Do you think to force her to accept of him?

ORGON

Yes, traitor, and this very evening, to plague you. Nay, I defy you all, and shall make you to know that I am master, and will be obeyed. Come, sirrah, do you recant; immediately throw yourself at his feet to beg his pardon.

DAMIS

Who, I? of this rascal, who by his impostures—

ORGON

What, scoundrel, do you rebel, and call him names? A cudgel there, a cudgel.

to Tartuffe

Don't hold me.

to his son

Get you out of my house this minute, and never dare to set foot into it again.

DAMIS

Yes, I shall go, but—

ORGON

Quickly, then, leave the place; sirrah, I disinherit thee, and give thee my curse besides.

exit Damis

To offend a holy person in such a manner!

TARTUFFE   *aside*

O Heaven! pardon him the anguish he gives me!

to Orgon

Could you know what a grief it is to me that they should try to blacken me with my dear brother—

ORGON

Alack-a-day!

TARTUFFE

The very thought of this ingratitude wounds me to the very quick!—

51

Lord, what horror!—My heart's so full that I can't speak; I think I shan't outlive it.

ORGON

running all in tears to the door out of which he drove his son

Villain! I'm sorry my hand spared, and did not make an end of thee on the spot.

to Tartuffe

Compose yourself, brother, and don't be troubled.

TARTUFFE

Let us by all means put an end to the course of these unhappy debates; I see what uneasiness I occasion here, and think there's a necessity, brother, for my leaving your house.

ORGON

How? You're not in earnest sure?

TARTUFFE

They hate me, and seek, I see, to bring my integrity into question with you.

ORGON

What signifies that? Do you see me listen to them?

TARTUFFE

They won't stop here, you may be sure; and those very stories which you now reject may one day meet with more credit.

ORGON

No, brother, never.

TARTUFFE

Ah! brother, a wife may easily deceive a husband.

ORGON

No, no.

TARTUFFE

Suffer me, by removing hence, immediately to remove from them all occasion of attacking me in this manner.

ORGON

No, you must stay, or it will cost me my life.

52

TARTUFFE

Well, then, I must mortify myself. If you would, however—

ORGON

Ah!

TARTUFFE

Be it so. Let's talk no more about it. But I know how I must behave on this occasion. Honour is delicate, and friendship obliges me to prevent reports and not to give any room for suspicion; I'll shun your wife, and you shall never see me—

ORGON

No, in spite of everybody, you shall frequently be with her. To vex the world is my greatest joy, and I'll have you seen with her at all hours. This is not all yet, the better to brave them. I'll have no other heir but you, and I'm going forthwith to sign you a deed of gift for my whole estate. A true and hearty friend, that I fix on for a son-in-law, is far dearer to me than either son, wife, or kindred. You won't refuse what I propose?

TARTUFFE

Heaven's will be done in all things.

ORGON

Poor man! Come, let's get the writings drawn up, and then let envy burst itself with spite.

ACT IV

Cléante, Tartuffe

CLÉANTE

Yes, 'tis in everybody's mouth, and you may believe me. The noise this rumour makes is not much to your credit; and I have met with you, sir, very opportunely, to tell you plainly, in two words, my thoughts of the matter. I shan't inquire into the ground of what's reported; I pass that by, and take the thing at worst. We'll suppose that Damis has not used you well, and that they have accused you wrongfully. Is it not the part of a good Christian to pardon the offence, and extinguish in his heart all desire of vengeance? Ought you to suffer a son to be turned out of his father's house on account of your differences? I tell you once again, and tell you frankly, there is neither small nor great but are scandalised at it. And if you take my advice, you'll make all up and not push matters to extremity. Sacrifice your resentment to your duty, and restore the son to his father's favour.

TARTUFFE

Alas! for my own part, I would do it with all my heart; I, sir, bear him not the least ill-will; I forgive him everything; I lay nothing to his charge, and would serve him with all my soul. But the interests of Heaven cannot admit of it: and if he comes in here again, I must go out. After such an unparalleled action, it would be scandalous for me to have anything to do with him. Heaven knows what all the world would immediately think on't. They would impute it to pure policy in me, and people would everywhere say that knowing myself guilty, I pretended a charitable zeal for my accuser; that I dreaded him at heart, and would practise upon him, that I might, underhand, engage him to silence.

CLÉANTE

You put us off here with sham excuses, and all your reasons, sir, are too far fetched. Why do you take upon you the interests of Heaven? Has it any occasion for our assistance in punishing the guilty? Leave, leave the care of its own vengeance to itself, and only think of that pardon of offences which it prescribes; have no regard to the judgment of men when you follow the sovereign orders of Heaven! What! shall the paltry interest of what people may believe, hinder the glory of a good action! No, no, let us always do what Heaven has prescribed, and perplex our heads with no other care.

TARTUFFE

I have told you already that I forgive him from my heart, and that is doing, sir, what Heaven ordains; but after the scandal and affront of to-day, Heaven does not require me to live with him.

CLÉANTE

And does it require you, sir, to lend an ear to what mere caprice dictates to the father? And to accept of an estate where justice obliges you to make no pretensions?

TARTUFFE

Those that know me will never have the thought that this is the effect of an interested spirit. All the riches of this world have few charms for me; I am not dazzled by their false glare, and if I should resolve to accept this present, which the father has a mind to make me, it is, to tell you the truth, only because I'm afraid this means will fall into wicked hands, lest it should come amongst such as will make an ill use on't in the world, and not lay it out, as I intend to do, for the glory of Heaven and the good of my neighbour.

CLÉANTE

Oh, entertain none of these very nice scruples, which may occasion the complaints of a right heir. Let him, without giving yourself any trouble, keep his estate at his own peril, and consider that 'twere better he misused it than that people should accuse you for depriving him of it. I only wonder, that you could receive such a proposal without confusion. For, in short, has true zeal any maxim which shows how to strip a lawful heir of his right? And if it must be that Heaven has put into your heart an invincible obstacle to living with Damis, would it not be better, like a man of prudence, that you should fairly retire from hence than thus to suffer the eldest son, contrary to all reason, to be turned out of doors for you? Believe me, sir, this would give your discretion—

TARTUFFE

It is half an hour past three, sir. Certain devotions call me above stairs, and you'll excuse my leaving you so soon.

alone

CLÉANTE

Ah!

enter Elmire,
Mariane and Dorine

to Cléante

DORINE

For goodness' sake, lend her what assistance you can, as we do. She's in the greatest perplexity, sir, imaginable; the articles her father has concluded for to-night make her every moment ready to despair. He's just a-coming; pray let us set on him in a body and try, either by force or cunning, to frustrate the unlucky design that has put us all into this consternation.

enter Orgon

ORGON

Hah! I'm glad to see you all together.

to Mariane

I bring something in this contract that will make you smile; you already know what this means.

kneeling to Orgon

MARIANE

Oh! sir, in the name of Heaven that is a witness of my grief, by everything that can move your heart, forgo a little the right nature has given you and dispense with my obedience in this particular. Don't compel me, by this hard law, to complain to Heaven of the duty I owe you. Do not, my father, render the life which you have given me unfortunate. If, contrary to the tender hopes I might have formed to myself, you won't suffer me to be the man's I presumed to love, at least, out of your goodness, which upon my knees I implore, save me from the torment of being the man's I abhor, and drive me not to despair by exerting your full power over me.

ORGON *aside*

Come, stand firm, my heart; no human weakness.

MARIANE

Your tenderness for him gives me no uneasiness. Show it in the strongest manner, give him your estate; and if that's not enough, add all mine to it; I consent with all my heart, and give it up; but at least go not so far as to my person. Suffer a convent, with its austerities, to wear out the mournful days allotted me by Heaven.

ORGON

Ay, these are exactly your she-devotees, when a father crosses their wanton inclinations. Get up, get up; the more it goes against you, the more you'll merit by it. Mortify your senses by this marriage, and don't din me in the head any more about it.

DORINE

But what—

ORGON

Hold your tongue; speak to your own concerns. I absolutely forbid you to open your lips.

CLÉANTE

If you would indulge me, in answer, to give one word of advice.

ORGON

Brother, your advice is the best in the world; 'tis very rational, and what I have a great value for. But you must not take it ill if I don't use it now.

ELMIRE *to Orgon*

Seeing what I see, I don't know what to say; I can but wonder at your blindness. You must be mightily bewitched and prepossessed in his favour, to give us the lie upon the fact of to-day.

ORGON

I am your humble servant, and believe appearances. I know your complaisance for my rascal of a son, and you were afraid to disavow the trick

57

he would have played the poor man. You were, in a word, too little ruffled to gain credit; you would have appeared to have been moved after a different manner.

ELMIRE

Is it requisite that our honour should bluster so vehemently at the simple declaration of an amorous transport? Can there be no reply made to what offends us, without fury in our eyes and invectives in our mouth? For my part, I only laugh at such overtures, and the rout made about them by no means pleases me. I love that we should show our discretion with good nature, and cannot like your savage prudes, whose honour is armed with teeth and claws and is for tearing a man's eyes out for a word speaking. Heaven preserve me from such discretion! I would have virtue that is not diabolical, and believe that a denial given with a discreet coldness is no less powerful to give the lover a rebuff.

ORGON

In short I know the whole affair, and shall not alter my scheme.

ELMIRE

I admire, still more, at your unaccountable weakness. But what answer could your incredulity make should one let you see that they told you the truth?

ORGON

See?

ELMIRE

Ay.

ORGON

Stuff!

ELMIRE

But how, if I should contrive a way to let you see it in a very clear light?

ORGON

A likely story indeed!

ELMIRE

What a strange man! At least give me an answer. I don't speak of your giving credit to us; but suppose a place could be found where you might see and overhear all, what would you then say of your good man?

ORGON

In that case, I should say that—I should say nothing, for the thing can't be.

ELMIRE

You have been too long deluded, and too much have taxed me with imposture. 'Tis necessary that by way of diversion, and without going any farther, I should make you a witness of all they told you.

ORGON

Do so; I take you at your word. We shall see your address, and how you'll make good your promise.

ELMIRE   *to Dorine*

Bid him come to me.

DORINE   *to Elmire*

He has a crafty soul of his own, and perhaps it would be a difficult matter to surprise him.

to Dorine

ELMIRE

No, people are easily duped by what they love, and self-love helps 'em to deceive themselves.

to Cléante and Mariane

Call him down to me, and do you retire.

exeunt Dorine, Cléante, Mariane

to Orgon

Now do you come and get under this table.

ORGON

Why so?

ELMIRE

'Tis a necessary point that you should be well concealed.

ORGON

But why under this table?

ELMIRE

Lack-a-day! do as I'd have you, I have my design in my head, and you shall be judge of it. Place yourself there, I tell you, and when you are there, take care that no one either sees or hears you.

ORGON

I must needs say, I am very complaisant: but I must see you go through your enterprise.

ELMIRE

You will have nothing, I believe, to reply to me.

to Orgon under the table

However, as I am going to touch upon a strange affair, don't be shocked by any means. Whatever I may say must be allowed me, as it is to convince you, according to my promise. I am going by coaxing speeches, since I am reduced to it, to make this hypocritical soul drop the mask, to flatter the impudent desires of his love, and give a full scope to his boldness. Since 'tis for your sake alone, and to confound him, that I feign a compliance with his desires, I may give over when you appear, and things need go no farther than you would have them. It lies on you to stop his mad pursuit when you think that matters are carried far enough, to spare your wife, and not to expose me any farther than is necessary to disabuse you. This is your interest, it lies at your discretion, and—He's coming; keep close, and take care not to appear.

enter Tartuffe

60

TARTUFFE

I was told you desired to speak with me here.

ELMIRE

Yes, I have secrets to discover to you; but pull to that door before I tell 'em you, and look about, for fear of a surprise.

Tartuffe goes and shuts the door and returns

We must not surely make such a business of it as the other was just now. I never was in such a surprise in my whole life: Damis put me into a terrible fright for you, and you saw very well that I did my utmost to baffle his designs and moderate his passion. I was under so much concern, 'tis true, that I had not the thought of contradicting him; but thanks to Heaven, everything was the better for that, and things are put upon a surer footing. The esteem you are in laid that storm, and my husband can have no suspicion of you. The better to set the rumour of ill tongues at defiance, he desires we should be always together, and from thence it is that without fear of blame I can be locked up with you here alone, and this is what justifies me in laying open to you a heart a little, perhaps, too forward in admitting of your passion.

TARTUFFE

This language, madame, is difficult enough to comprehend, and you talked in another kind of style but just now.

ELMIRE

Alas! if such a refusal disobliges you, how little do you know the heart of a woman! and how little do you know what it means when we make so feeble a defence! Our modesty will always combat, in these moments, those tender sentiments you may inspire us with. Whatever reason we may find for the passion that subdues us, we shall always be a little ashamed to own it. We defend ourselves at first, but by the air with which we go about it, we give you sufficiently to know that our heart surrenders, that our words oppose our wishes for the sake of honour, and that such refusals promise everything. Without doubt this is making a very free confession to you, and having regard little enough to the modesty that belongs to us; but in short, since the word has slipped me, should I have been bent so much upon restraining Damis? Should I, pray, with so much mildness, have hearkened to the offer at large which you made of your heart? Should I have taken the thing as you saw I did, if the offer of your heart had had nothing in it to please me? And when I myself would have forced you to refuse the match which had just been proposed, what is it this instance should have given you to understand but the interest one was inclined to take in you, and the disquiet it would have given me, that the knot resolved on should at least divide a heart which I wanted to have wholly my own?

61

TARTUFFE

'Tis no doubt, madame, an extreme pleasure to hear these words from the lips one loves; their honey plentifully diffuses through every sense a sweetness I never before tasted. My supreme study is the happiness of pleasing you, and my heart counts your affection its beatitude; but you must excuse this heart, madame, if it presumes to doubt a little of its felicity. I can fancy these words to be only a sort of artifice to make me break off the match that's upon the conclusion; and if I may with freedom explain myself to you, I shall not rely upon this so tender language till some of the favours which I sigh after, assure me of the sincerity of what may be said, and fix in my mind a firm belief of the transporting goodness you intend me.

ELMIRE

coughing to give her husband notice

What! proceed so fast? Would you exhaust the tenderness of one's heart at once? One does violence to one's self in making you the most melting

62

declaration; but at the same time this is not enough for you, and one cannot advance so far as to satisfy you unless one pushes the affair to the last favours.

TARTUFFE

The less one deserves a blessing, the less one presumes to hope for it; our love can hardly have a full reliance upon discourses; one easily suspects a condition full fraught with happiness, and one would enjoy it before one believes it. For my particular, who know I so little deserve your favours, I doubt the success of my rashness, and I shall believe nothing, madame, till by realities you have convinced my passion.

ELMIRE

Good lack! how your love plays the very tyrant! What a strange confusion it throws me into! With what a furious sway does it govern the heart! and with what violence it pushes for what it desires! What, is there no getting clear of your pursuit? Do you allow one no time to take breath? Is it decent to persist with so great rigour? To insist upon the things you demand without quarter? To abuse in this manner, by your pressing efforts, the foible you see people have for you?

TARTUFFE

But if you regard my addresses with a favourable eye, why do you refuse me convincing proofs of it?

ELMIRE

But how can one comply with your desires without offending that Heaven which you are always talking of?

TARTUFFE

If nothing but Heaven obstructs my wishes, 'tis a trifle with me to remove such an obstacle, and that need be no restraint upon your love.

ELMIRE

But they so terrify us with the judgments of Heaven!

TARTUFFE

I can dissipate those ridiculous terrors for you, madame; I have the knack of easing scruples. Heaven, 'tis true, forbids certain gratifications. But then there are ways of compounding those matters. It is a science to stretch the strings of conscience according to the different exigences of the case, and to rectify the immorality of the action by the purity of our intention. These are secrets, madame, I can instruct you in; you have nothing to do but passively to be conducted. Satisfy my desire, and fear nothing; I'll answer for you, and will take the sin upon myself.

Elmire coughs loud

You cough very much, madame.

ELMIRE

Yes, I am on the rack.

*presenting her with
a paper*

TARTUFFE

Will you please to have a bit of this liquorice?

ELMIRE

'Tis an obstinate cold, without doubt, and I am satisfied that all the liquorice in the world will do no good in this case.

TARTUFFE

It is, to be sure, very troublesome.

ELMIRE

Ay, more than one can express.

TARTUFFE

In short your scruple, madame, is easily overcome. You are sure of its being an inviolable secret here, and the harm never consists in anything but the noise one makes; the scandal of the world is what makes the offence, and sinning in private is no sinning at all.

ELMIRE

*after coughing again,
and striking upon
the table*

In short, I see that I must resolve to yield, that I must consent to grant you everything, and that with less than this I ought not to expect that you should be satisfied or give over. It is indeed very hard to go that length, and I get over it much against my will. But since you are obstinately bent upon reducing me to it, and since you won't believe anything that can be said, but still insist on more convincing testimony, one must e'en resolve upon it and satisfy people. And if this gratification carries any offence in it, so much the worse for him who forces me to this violence; the fault certainly ought not to be laid at my door.

TARTUFFE

Yes, madame, I take it upon myself, and the thing in itself—

ELMIRE

Open the door a little, and pray look if my husband be not in that gallery.

TARTUFFE

What need you take so much care about him? Betwixt us two, he's a man to be led by the nose. He will take a pride in all our conversations, and I have wrought him up to the point of seeing everything without believing anything.

ELMIRE

That signifies nothing; pray go out a little, and look carefully all about.

exit Tartuffe

ORGON

coming from under the table

An abominable fellow, I vow! I can't recover myself; this perfectly stuns me.

ELMIRE

How! do you come out so soon? You make fools of people; get under the table again, stay to the very last, to see things sure, and don't trust to bare conjectures.

ORGON

No, nothing more wicked ever came from Hell.

ELMIRE

Dear heart, you must not believe too lightly; suffer yourself to be fully convinced before you yield, and don't be too hasty for fear of a mistake.

Elmire places Orgon behind her enter Tartuffe

TARTUFFE

not seeing Orgon

Everything conspires, madame, to my satisfaction. I have surveyed this whole apartment; nobody's there, and my ravished soul—

Tartuffe going with open arms to embrace Elmire, she retires, and Tartuffe sees Orgon

ORGON

stopping Tartuffe

Gently, gently; you are too eager in your amours; you should not be so furious. Ah, ha, good man! you intended me a crest, I suppose! Good-lack,

65

how you abandon yourself to temptations! What, you'd marry my daughter, and had a huge stomach to my wife? I was a long while in doubt whether all was in good earnest, and always thought you would change your tone; but this is pushing the proof far enough. I am now satisfied, and want, for my part, no further conviction.

ELMIRE

to Tartuffe

The part I have played was contrary to my inclination; but they reduced me to the necessity of treating you in this manner.

TARTUFFE

to Orgon

What? Do you believe—

ORGON

Come, pray no noise; turn out, and without ceremony.

TARTUFFE

My design—

ORGON

These speeches are no longer in season; you must troop off forthwith.

TARTUFFE

'Tis you must troop off, you who speak so magisterially. The house belongs to me; I'll make you know it, and shall plainly show you that you have recourse in vain to these base tricks to pick a quarrel with me; that you don't think where you are when you injure me; that I have wherewithal to confound and punish imposture, to avenge offended Heaven, and make them repent it who talk here of turning me out o' doors.

exit Tartuffe

ELMIRE

What language is this? And what can it mean?

ORGON

In truth I'm all confusion, and have no room to laugh.

ELMIRE

How so?

ORGON

I see my fault by what he says, and the deed of gift perplexes me.

66

ELMIRE
The deed of gift?

ORGON
Ay, 'tis done; but I have something else that disturbs me too.

ELMIRE
And what's that?

ORGON
You shall know the whole; but let's go immediately and see if a certain casket is above stairs.

67

ACT V

Enter Orgon, Cléante

CLÉANTE
Whither would you run?

ORGON
Alas! how can I tell?

CLÉANTE
I think we ought, the first thing we do, to consult together what may be done at this juncture.

ORGON
This casket entirely confounds me. It gives me even more vexation than all the rest.

CLÉANTE
This casket then is some mystery of importance?

ORGON

It is a deposit that Argas, my lamented friend, himself committed as a great secret to my keeping. When he fled, he pitched on me for this purpose; and these are the papers, as he told me, whereon his life and fortune depend.

CLÉANTE

Why then did you trust them in other hands?

ORGON

Merely out of a scruple of conscience. I went straight to impart the secret to my traitor, and his casuistry over-persuaded me rather to give him the casket to keep; so that to deny it, in case of any inquiry, I might have the relief of a subterfuge ready at hand, whereby my conscience would have been very secure in taking an oath contrary to the truth.

CLÉANTE

You are in a bad situation, at least, if I may believe appearances; both the deed of gift and the trust reposed are, to speak my sentiments to you, steps which you have taken very inconsiderately. One might carry you great lengths by such pledges; and this fellow having these advantages over you, it is still a great imprudence in you to urge him; and you ought to think of some gentler method.

ORGON

What! under the fair appearance of such affectionate zeal, to conceal such a double heart, and a soul so wicked? And that I, who took him in poor and indigent—'Tis over, I renounce all pious folks. I shall henceforth have an utter abhorrence of them, and shall become, for their sakes, worse than a devil.

CLÉANTE

Mighty well; here are some of your extravagances! You never preserve a moderate temper in anything. Right reason and yours are very different, and you are always throwing yourself out of one extreme into another. You see your error and are sensible that you have been imposed on by a hypocritical zeal; but in order to reform, what reason is there that you should be guilty of a worse mistake, and that you should make no difference between the heart of a perfidious worthless wretch and those of all honest people? What! because a rascal has impudently imposed upon you under the pompous show of an austere grimace, will you needs have it that everybody's like him, and that there are no devout people to be found in the world? Leave these foolish consequences to libertines; distinguish between virtue and the appearance of it; never hazard your esteem too suddenly; and, in order to do this, keep the mean you should do. Guard, if possible, against doing honour to imposture; but, at the same time, don't injure true zeal; and if you must fall into one extreme, rather offend again on the other side.

enter Damis

DAMIS

What, sir, is it true that the rascal threatens you? That he has quite forgotten every favour he has received? And that his base abominable pride arms your own goodness against yourself?

ORGON

Yes, son, and it gives me inconceivable vexation.

DAMIS

Let me alone, I'll slice both his ears off. There's no dallying with such insolence as his. I'll undertake to rid you of your fears at once; and to put an end to the affair, I must do his business for him.

CLÉANTE

That's spoken exactly like a young fellow. Pray moderate these violent transports; we live in an age, and under a government, in which violence is but a bad way to promote our affairs.

enter Mme Pernelle,
Elmire, Mariane,
Dorine

Mme PERNELLE

What's all this? I hear terrible mysteries here.

ORGON

They are novelties that I am an eye-witness to; you see how finely I am fitted for my care. I kindly pick up a fellow in misery, entertain and treat him like my own brother, heap daily favours on him; I give him my daughter and my whole fortune; when at the same time the perfidious, infamous wretch forms the black design of seducing my wife. And not content with these base attempts, he dares to menace me with my own favours, and would make use of those advantages to my ruin which my too indiscreet good-nature put into his hands, to turn me out of my estate, which I made over to him, and to reduce me to that condition from which I rescued him.

DORINE

The poor man!

Mme PERNELLE

I can never believe, son, he could commit so black an action.

ORGON
How?

Mme PERNELLE
Good people are always envied.

ORGON
What would you insinuate, mother, by this discourse?

Mme PERNELLE
Why, that there are strange doings at your house; and the ill-will they bear him is but too evident.

ORGON
What has this ill-will to do with what has been told you?

Mme PERNELLE
I have told you a hundred times when you were a little one,

That virtue here is persecuted ever;
That envious men may die, but envy never.

ORGON

But what is all this to the present purpose?

Mme PERNELLE

They have trumped up to you a hundred idle stories against him.

ORGON

I have told you already that I saw it all my own self.

Mme PERNELLE

The malice of scandal-mongers is very great.

ORGON

You'll make me swear, mother. I tell you that I saw with my own eyes a crime so audacious—

Mme PERNELLE

Tongues never want for venom to spit; nothing here below can be proof against them.

ORGON

This is holding a very senseless argument! I saw it, I say, saw it; with my own eyes I saw it. What you call, saw it. Must I din it a hundred times into your ears, and bawl as loud as four folks?

Mme PERNELLE

Dear heart! Appearances very often deceive us. You must not always judge by what you see.

ORGON

I shall run mad.

Mme PERNELLE

Nature is liable to false suspicions, and good is oftentimes misconstrued evil.

ORGON

Ought I to construe charitably his desire of kissing my wife?

Mme PERNELLE

You ought never to accuse anybody but upon good grounds; and you should have stayed till you had seen the thing certain.

72

ORGON

What the devil! How should I be more certain? Then, mother, I should have stayed till he had—You'll make me say some foolish thing or other.

Mme PERNELLE

In short, his soul burns with too pure a flame, and I can't let it enter my thoughts that he could attempt the things that are laid to his charge.

ORGON

Go, if you were not my mother I don't know what I might say to you, my passion is so great!

DORINE *to Orgon*

The just return, sir, of things here below. Time was, you would believe nobody, and now you can't be believed yourself.

CLÉANTE

We are wasting that time in mere trifles which should be spent in taking measures; we shouldn't sleep when a knave threatens.

DAMIS

What, can his impudence come to this pitch?

ELMIRE

I can scarce think this instance possible, for my part; his ingratitude would in this be too visible.

CLÉANTE *to Orgon*

Don't you depend upon that. He will be cunning enough to give the colour of reason for what he does against you; and for a less matter than this, the weight of a cabal has involved people in dismal labyrinths. I tell you once again that, armed with what he has, you should never have urged him so far.

ORGON

That's true; but what could I do in the affair? I was not master of my resentments at the haughtiness of the traitor.

CLÉANTE

I wish with all my heart that there could be any shadow of a peace patched up between you.

73

ELMIRE

Had I but known how well he had been armed, I should never have made such an alarm about the matter, and my—

to Dorine, seeing M. Loyal coming

ORGON

What would that man have? Go quickly and ask. I'm in a fine condition to have people come to see me.

enter M. Loyal

M. LOYAL

to Dorine at the farther part of the stage

Good-morrow, child; pray let me speak to your master.

DORINE

He's in company, and I doubt he can see nobody now.

M. LOYAL

Nay, I am not for being troublesome here. I believe my coming will have nothing in it that will displease him; I come upon an affair that he'll be very glad of.

DORINE

Your name, pray?

M. LOYAL

Only tell him that I come on the part of Monsieur Tartuffe, for his good.

DORINE   *to Orgon*

'Tis a man who comes in a civil way upon business from Monsieur Tartuffe, which he says you won't dislike.

CLÉANTE   *to Orgon*

You must see who this man is and what he wants.

ORGON   *to Cléante*

Perhaps he comes to make us friends. How shall I behave myself to him?

CLÉANTE

Be sure don't be angry, and if he speaks of an agreement you must listen to him.

M. LOYAL   *to Orgon*

Save you, sir! Heaven blast the man who would wrong you, and may it be as favourable to you as I wish.

ORGON   *aside to Cléante*

This mild beginning favours my conjecture, and already forebodes some accommodation.

M. LOYAL

I always had a prodigious value for all your family, and was servant to the gentleman your father.

ORGON

Sir, I am much ashamed, and ask pardon that I don't know you or your name.

75

M. LOYAL

My name is Loyal, sir, by birth a Norman, and I am tipstaff to the court in spite of envy. I have had the good fortune for forty years together to fill that office, thanks to Heaven, with great honour. I come, sir, with your leave, to signify to you the execution of a certain decree.

ORGON

What, are you here—

M. LOYAL

Sir, without passion, 'tis nothing but a summons, an order to remove hence, you and yours, to take out your goods, and to make way for others, without remission or delay, so that 'tis necessary—

ORGON

I go from hence?

M. LOYAL

Yes, sir, if you please. The house at present, as you know but too well, belongs to good Monsieur Tartuffe, without dispute. He is henceforward lord and master of your estate, by virtue of a contract I have in charge. 'Tis in due form, and not to be contested.

to M. Loyal

DAMIS

Most certainly 'tis prodigious impudence, and what I can't but admire!

to Damis

M. LOYAL

Sir, my business is not with you but

pointing to Orgon

with this gentleman, who is mild and reasonable, and knows the duty of an honest man too well to oppose authority.

ORGON

But—

to Orgon

M. LOYAL

Yes, sir, I know you would not rebel for a million, and that, like a good honest gentleman, you will suffer me here to execute the orders I have received.

DAMIS

You may chance, Monsieur Tipstaff, to get your black jacket well brushed here.

M. LOYAL *to Orgon*

Either, sir, cause your son to be silent or withdraw. I should be very loath to put pen to paper, and see your names in my information.

DORINE *aside*

This Monsieur Loyal has a disloyal sort of look with him!

M. LOYAL

I have a great deal of tenderness for all honest people, and should not, sir, have charged myself with these writs but to serve and oblige you and to prevent another's being pitched on, who, not having the love for you which I have, might have proceeded in a less gentle manner.

ORGON

And what can be worse than to order people to go out of their house?

M. LOYAL

Why, you are allowed time. And, till to-morrow, I shall suspend, sir, the execution of the warrant. I shall only come and pass the night here with half a score of my folks, without noise or scandal. For form's sake, if you please, the keys of the door must, before you go to bed, be brought me. I'll take care your rest shan't be disturbed, and suffer nothing that is improper to be done. But to-morrow morning you must be ready to clear the house of even the least utensil. My people shall assist you, and I have picked out a set of lusty fellows that they may do you the more service in your removal. Nobody can use you better, in my opinion; and as I treat you with great indulgence, I conjure you, sir, to make a good use of it and to give me no disturbance in the execution of my office.

ORGON *aside*

I'd give just now a hundred of the best louis d'ors I have left, for the power and pleasure of laying one sound blow on your ass-ship's muzzle.

CLÉANTE *aside to Orgon*

Give over; don't let's make things worse.

DAMIS

This impudence is too great; I can hardly refrain; my fingers itch to be at him.

DORINE

Faith, Monsieur Brawny-backed Loyal, some thwacks of a cudgel would by no means sit ill upon you.

M. LOYAL

Those infamous words are punishable, sweetheart; there's law against women too.

to M. Loyal

CLÉANTE

Let us come to a conclusion, sir, with this; 'tis enough. Pray give up your paper of indulgence and leave us.

M. LOYAL

Good-bye to ye. Heaven bless you all together!

ORGON

And confound both thee and him that sent thee!

exit M. Loyal

Well, mother, you see whether I am in the right or no; and you may judge of the rest by the warrant. Do you at length perceive his treacheries?

Mme PERNELLE

I am stunned, and am tumbling from the clouds.

to Orgon

DORINE

You complain without a cause, and blame him wrongfully; this does but confirm his pious intentions. His virtue is made perfect in the love of his neighbour; he knows, very often, that riches spoil the man; and he would only, out of pure charity, take from you everything that may obstruct your salvation.

ORGON

Hold your tongue. Must I always be repeating that to you?

to Orgon

CLÉANTE

Come, let's consult what's proper for you to do.

ELMIRE

Go and expose the audaciousness of the ungrateful wretch. This proceeding of his invalidates the contract; and his perfidiousness must needs appear too black to let him have the success we are apt to surmise.

enter Valère

VALÈRE

'Tis with regret, sir, I come to afflict you, but I am constrained to it by the imminence of the danger. A very intimate friend of mine, who knows the interest I ought to take in everything that may concern you, has for my sake violated, by a delicate step, the secrecy due to the affairs of state, and has just sent me advice, the consequence of which reduces you to the expedient of a sudden flight. The rogue who has long imposed on you has thought fit, an hour ago, to accuse you to your prince, and to put into his hands, among other darts he shoots at you, the important casket of a state-criminal, of which, says he, in contempt of the duty of a subject, you have kept the guilty secret. I am not informed of the detail of the crime laid to your charge, but an order is issued out against your person, and to execute it the better, he himself is appointed to accompany the person that is to arrest you.

79

CLÉANTE

Now are his pretensions armed, and this is the way that the traitor seeks to make himself master of your estate.

ORGON

The man, I must own, is a vile animal!

VALÈRE

The least delay may be fatal to you; I have my coach at the door to carry you off, with a thousand louis d'ors that here I bring you. Let's lose no time; the shaft is thrown, and these blows are only parried by flight. I offer myself to conduct you to a place of safety and to accompany you in your escape, even to the last.

ORGON

Alas, what do I not owe to your obliging care! I must take another time to thank you, and I beseech Heaven to be so propitious to me that I may one day acknowledge this generous service. Farewell! Take care, the rest of you—

CLÉANTE

Go quickly; we shall take care, brother, to do what is proper.

enter Tartuffe and a Police Officer

stopping Orgon

TARTUFFE

Softly, sir, softly, don't run so fast, you shan't go far to find you a lodging; we take you prisoner in the king's name.

ORGON

Traitor, thou hast reserved this shaft for the last. 'Tis the stroke by which thou art to dispatch me, and this crowns all the rest of thy perfidies.

TARTUFFE

Your abuses have nothing in them that can incense me; I'm instructed to suffer everything for the sake of Heaven.

CLÉANTE

The moderation is great, I must confess.

DAMIS

How impudently the varlet sports with Heaven!

TARTUFFE

All your raving can't move me; I think of nothing but doing my duty.

MARIANE

You have much glory to expect from hence; this employ is a mighty honourable one for you.

TARTUFFE

The employ can't be other than glorious when it proceeds from the power that sent me hither.

ORGON

But do you remember, ungrateful wretch, that my charitable hand raised you from a miserable condition?

TARTUFFE

Yes, I know what succours I might receive from thence, but the interest of my prince is my highest duty. The just obligation whereof stifles in my heart all other acknowledgments; and I could sacrifice to so powerful a tie, friend, wife, kindred, and myself to boot.

ELMIRE

The hypocrite!

DORINE

How artfully he can make a cloak of what is sacred!

CLÉANTE

But if the zeal that puts you on, and with which you trick yourself out, is so perfect as you say it is, how came it not to show itself till he found means of surprising you soliciting his wife? How came you not to think of informing against him till his honour obliged him to drive you out of his house? I don't say that the making over his whole estate to you lately should draw you from your duty; but intending to treat him, as now you do, like a criminal, why did you consent to take anything from him?

TARTUFFE *to the Officer*

I beg you, sir, to free me from this clamour, and be pleased to do as you are ordered.

OFFICER

Yes, 'tis certainly delaying the execution too long. You invite me to fulfil it apropos; and to execute my order, follow me immediately to the prison which we are to allot you for your habitation.

TARTUFFE

Who? I, sir?

81

OFFICER
Yes, you.

TARTUFFE
Why to prison, pray?

OFFICER
You are not the person I shall give an account to.

to Orgon

Do you, sir, compose yourself after so warm a surprise. We live under a prince who is an enemy to fraud, a prince whose eyes penetrate into the heart, and whom all the art of impostors can't deceive. His great soul is furnished with a fine discernment, and always takes things in a right light; there's nothing gets too much footing by surprise, and his solid reason falls into no excess. He bestows lasting glory on men of worth, but he dispenses his favours without blindness, and his love for the sincere does not foreclose his heart against the horror that's due to those that are otherwise. Even this person was not able to surprise him, and we find he keeps clear of the most subtle snares. He soon pierced through all the baseness contained within his heart. Coming to accuse you, he betrayed himself; and by a just stroke of divine judgment, he discovered himself to be a notorious rogue, of whom His Majesty had received information under another name, the whole detail of whose horrid crimes is long enough to fill volumes of histories. This monarch, in a word, detesting his ingratitude and undutifulness to you, to his other confusions hath added the following, and hath sent me under his direction only to see how far his assurance would carry him and to oblige him to give you full satisfaction. He wills moreover that I should strip the traitor of all your papers to which he pretends a right, and give them you. By dint of sovereign power he dissolves the obligation of the contract which gives him your estate, and he pardons moreover this secret offence in which the retreat of your friend involved you; and this recompense he bestows for the zeal he saw you formerly showed in maintaining his rights. To let you see that his heart knows, even when 'tis least expected, how to recompense a good action; that merit with him is never lost, and that he much better remembers good than evil.

DORINE
May Heaven be praised!

Mme PERNELLE
Now I begin to revive.

ELMIRE
Favourable success!

MARIANE

Who could have foretold this?

ORGON

Well, traitor, there you are—

to Tartuffe as the
Officer leads him off

exit the Officer with
Tartuffe

CLÉANTE

Nay, brother, hold, and don't descend to indignities; leave the wretch to his evil destiny, and don't add to the remorse that oppresses him. Much rather wish that his heart may now happily become a convert to virtue, that he may reform his life through detestation of his crimes, and may soften the justice of a glorious prince; while for his goodness you go and on your knees make the due returns for his lenity to you.

ORGON

Yes, 'tis well said. Let us, with joy, go throw ourselves at his royal feet, to glory in the goodness which he generously displays to us; then, having acquitted ourselves of this first duty, 'twill be necessary we should apply ourselves, with just care, to another:

> *With Hymen's tend'rest joys to crown Valère—*
> *The generous lover, and the friend sincere.*

THE
WOULD-BE GENTLEMAN

Le Bourgeois Gentilhomme

ACTORS

M. JOURDAIN   *the bourgeois*

MME JOURDAIN   *wife to M. Jourdain*

LUCILE   *daughter to M. Jourdain*

CLÉONTE   *in love with Lucile*

DORIMÈNE   *a marchioness*

DORANTE   *a count, Dorimène's lover*

NICOLE   *a maid-servant to M. Jourdain*

COVIELLE   *servant to Cléonte*

MUSIC MASTER

MUSIC MASTER'S PUPIL

DANCING MASTER

FENCING MASTER

PHILOSOPHY MASTER

MASTER TAILOR

JOURNEYMAN TAILOR

LACKEYS

The Scene is Paris, in M. Jourdain's house

ACT I

Music Master, a Pupil of the Music Master
(composing at a table in the middle of the stage), a Woman Singer,
and two Men Singers; a Dancing Master and Dancers

MUSIC MASTER *to the musicians*

Here, step into this hall, and sit there till he comes.

DANCING MASTER *to the dancers*

And you too, on this side.

MUSIC MASTER *to his pupil*

Is it done?

PUPIL
Yes.

MUSIC MASTER

Let's see. . . . 'Tis mighty well.

DANCING MASTER

Is it anything new?

MUSIC MASTER

Yes, 'tis an air for a serenade, which I set him to compose here while we wait till our gentleman's awake.

DANCING MASTER

May one see what it is?

MUSIC MASTER

You will hear it, with the dialogue, when he comes. He won't be long.

DANCING MASTER

We have no want of business, either of us, at present.

MUSIC MASTER

'Tis true. We have found a man here, just such a one as we both of us want. This same Monsieur Jourdain is a sweet income, with his visions of nobility and gallantry which he has got into his noddle, and it would be well for your capers and my crotchets, were all the world like him.

DANCING MASTER

Not altogether so well; I wish, for his sake, that he were better skilled than he is in the things we give him.

MUSIC MASTER

It is true he understands 'em ill, but he pays for 'em well. And that's what our art has more need of at present than of anything else.

DANCING MASTER

For my part, I own it to you, I regale a little upon glory. I am sensible of applause, and think it a very grievous punishment in the liberal arts to display one's self to fools and to expose our compositions to the barbarous judgment of the stupid. Talk no more of it, there is a pleasure in working for persons who are capable of relishing the delicacies of an art, who know how to give a kind reception to the beauties of a work, and, by titillating approbation, regale you for your labour. Yes, the most agreeable recompense one can receive for the things one does is to see them understood, to see 'em caressed with an applause that does you honour. There's nothing, in my opinion, which pays us better than this for all our fatigues. And the praises of connoisseurs give an exquisite delight.

MUSIC MASTER

I grant it, and I relish them as well as you. There is nothing certainly that tickles more than the applause you speak of, but one cannot live upon this incense. Sheer praises won't make a man easy. There must be something solid mixed withal, and the best method of praising is to praise with the open hand. This indeed is one whose understanding is very shallow, who speaks of everything awry, and cross of the grain, and never applauds but in contradiction to sense. But his money sets his judgment right. He has discernment in his purse. His praises are current coin; and this ignorant commoner is more worth to us, as you see, than that grand witty lord who introduced us here.

DANCING MASTER

There's something of truth in what you say; but I find you lean a little too much towards the pelf. And mere interest is something so base that an honest man should never discover an attachment to it.

MUSIC MASTER

For all that, you decently receive the money our spark gives you.

DANCING MASTER

Certainly; but I don't place all my happiness in that: and I wish that, with his fortune, he had also some good taste of things.

89

MUSIC MASTER

I wish the same; 'tis what we both labour at as much as we can. But, however, he gives us the opportunity of making ourselves known in the world;
and he'll pay for others what others praise for him.

DANCING MASTER

Here he comes.

*enter
M. Jourdain
(in a nightgown and cap)
and two Lackeys*

M. JOURDAIN

Well, gentlemen? What have you there? Will you let me see your little
drollery?

DANCING MASTER

How? What little drollery?

M. JOURDAIN

Why the—how do you call that thing? your prologue, or dialogue of songs
and dancing.

DANCING MASTER

Ha, ha!

MUSIC MASTER

You see we are ready.

M. JOURDAIN

I have made you wait a little, but 'tis because I am to be dressed out to-day
like your people of quality; and my hosier has sent me a pair of silk stockings
which I thought I should never have got on.

MUSIC MASTER

We are here only to wait your leisure.

M. JOURDAIN

I desire you'll both stay till they have brought me my clothes, that you may
see me.

DANCING MASTER

As you please.

M. JOURDAIN
You shall see me most exactly equipped from head to foot.

MUSIC MASTER
We don't doubt it.

M. JOURDAIN
I have had this Indian thing made up for me.

DANCING MASTER
'Tis very handsome.

M. JOURDAIN
My tailor tells me that people of quality go thus in a morning.

MUSIC MASTER
It fits you to a miracle.

M. JOURDAIN
Why, ho! Fellow there! both my fellows!

FIRST LACKEY
Your pleasure, sir?

M. JOURDAIN

Nothing! 'Tis only to try whether you hear me readily.
to the Music and Dancing Masters
What say you of
my liveries?

DANCING MASTER
They are magnificent.

M. JOURDAIN

half-opens his gown and reveals a tight pair of breeches of scarlet velvet, and a green velvet jacket

Here again is a kind of dishabille to perform my exercises in a morning.

MUSIC MASTER
'Tis gallant.

91

M. JOURDAIN
Lackey!

FIRST LACKEY
Sir?

M. JOURDAIN
T'other lackey!

SECOND LACKEY
Sir?

taking off his gown

M. JOURDAIN

Hold my gown.
to the Music and Dancing Masters
Do you like me so?

DANCING MASTER
Mighty well; nothing can be better.

M. JOURDAIN
Now for your affair a little.

MUSIC MASTER
I should be glad first to let you hear an air
pointing to his pupil
he has just composed for the
serenade which you gave me orders about. He is one of my pupils, who has
an admirable talent for these sort of things.

M. JOURDAIN
Yes, but that should not have been put to a pupil to do; you were not too
good for that business yourself.

MUSIC MASTER
You must not let the name of pupil impose upon you, sir. These sort of
pupils know as much as the greatest masters, and the air is as good as can
be made. Hear it only.

to his servants

M. JOURDAIN

Give me my gown that I may hear the better.—Stay, I believe I shall be
better without the gown.—No, give it me again, it will do better.

92

MUSICIAN

I languish night and day, nor sleeps my pain,
Since those fair eyes imposed the rigorous chain;
But tell me, Iris, what dire fate attends
Your enemies, if thus you treat your friends?

M. JOURDAIN

This song seems to me a little upon the dismal; it inclines one to sleep; I should be glad you could enliven it a little here and there.

MUSIC MASTER

'Tis necessary, sir, that the air should be suited to the words.

M. JOURDAIN

I was taught one perfectly pretty some time ago. Stay—um—how is it?

DANCING MASTER

In good troth, I don't know.

M. JOURDAIN

There's lamb in it.

DANCING MASTER

Lamb?

M. JOURDAIN

Yes—Ho!

I thought my dear Namby
As gentle as fair-o:
I thought my dear Namby
As mild as a lamb-y.
Oh dear, oh dear, oh dear-o!
For now the sad scold is a thousand times told,
More fierce than a tiger or bear-o.

Isn't it pretty?

MUSIC MASTER

The prettiest in the world.

DANCING MASTER

And you sing it well.

M. JOURDAIN
Yet I never learnt music.

MUSIC MASTER
You ought to learn it, sir, as you do dancing. They are two arts which have a strict connection one with the other.

DANCING MASTER
And which open the human mind to see the beauty of things.

M. JOURDAIN
What, do people of quality learn music too?

MUSIC MASTER
Yes, sir.

M. JOURDAIN
I'll learn it then. But I don't know how I shall find time. For, besides the fencing master who teaches me, I have also got me a philosophy master, who is to begin this morning.

MUSIC MASTER
Philosophy is something; but music, sir, music—

DANCING MASTER
Music and dancing—music and dancing, that is all that's necessary.

MUSIC MASTER
There's nothing so profitable in a state as music.

DANCING MASTER
There's nothing so necessary for men as dancing.

MUSIC MASTER
A state cannot subsist without music.

DANCING MASTER
Without dancing, a man can do nothing.

MUSIC MASTER
All the disorders, all the wars one sees in the world, happen only from not learning music.

DANCING MASTER
All the disasters of mankind, all the fatal misfortunes that histories are re-

plete with, the blunders of politicians, the miscarriages of great commanders, all this comes from want of skill in dancing.

M. JOURDAIN
How so?

MUSIC MASTER
Does not war proceed from want of concord amongst men?

M. JOURDAIN
That's true.

MUSIC MASTER
And if all men learnt music, would not that be a means of keeping them better in tune, and of seeing universal peace in the world?

M. JOURDAIN
You're in the right.

DANCING MASTER
When a man has been guilty of a defect in his conduct—be it in the affairs of his family, or in the government of the state, or in the command of an army—don't we always say, such a one has made a false step in such an affair?

M. JOURDAIN
Yes, we say so.

DANCING MASTER
And can making a false step proceed from anything but not knowing how to dance?

M. JOURDAIN
'Tis true, and you are both in the right.

DANCING MASTER
This is to let you see the excellence and advantage of dancing and music.

M. JOURDAIN
I now comprehend it.

MUSIC MASTER
Will you see each of our compositions?

M. JOURDAIN
Yes.

MUSIC MASTER

I have told you already that this is a slight essay which I formerly made upon the different passions that may be expressed by music.

M. JOURDAIN

Very well.

to the musicians

MUSIC MASTER

Here, come forward.

to M. Jourdain

You are to imagine with yourself that they are dressed like shepherds.

M. JOURDAIN

Why always shepherds? One sees nothing but such stuff everywhere.

MUSIC MASTER

When we are to introduce persons as speaking in music, 'tis necessary to probability that we give in to the pastoral way. Singing has always been appropriated to shepherds; and it is by no means natural in dialogue that princes or citizens should sing their passions.

M. JOURDAIN

Be it so, be it so. Let's see.

dialogue in music between a Woman and two Men

WOMAN

The heart that must tyrannic love obey,
A thousand fears and cares oppress.
Sweet are those sighs and languishments, they say;
Say what they will for me,
Nought is so sweet as liberty.

FIRST MAN

Nothing so sweet as love's soft fire,
Which can two glowing hearts inspire
With the same life, the same desire.
The loveless swain no happiness can prove.
From life take soothing love,
All pleasure you remove.

SECOND MAN

Sweet were the wanton archer's sway,
Would all with constancy obey;
But, cruel fate!
No nymph is true:
The faithless sex more worthy of our hate,
To love should bid eternally adieu.

FIRST MAN

Pleasing heat!

WOMAN

Freedom blest!

SECOND MAN

Fair deceit!

FIRST MAN

O how I love thee!

WOMAN

How I approve thee!

SECOND MAN

I detest!

FIRST MAN

Against love's ardour quit this mortal hate.

WOMAN

Shepherd, myself I bind here,
To show a faithful mate.

SECOND MAN

Alas! but where to find her?

WOMAN

Our glory to retrieve,
My heart I here bestow.

SECOND MAN

But, nymph, can I believe
That heart no change will know?

WOMAN

Let experience decide,
Who loves best of the two.

SECOND MAN

And the perjured side
May vengeance pursue.

ALL THREE

Then let us kindle soft desire,
Let us fan the amorous fire.
Ah! how sweet it is to love,
When hearts united constant prove!

M. JOURDAIN
Is this all?

MUSIC MASTER
Yes.

M. JOURDAIN
I find 'tis very concise, and there are some little sayings in it pretty enough.

DANCING MASTER
You have here, for my composition, a little essay of the finest movements, and the most beautiful attitudes with which a dance can possibly be varied.

M. JOURDAIN
Are they shepherds too?

DANCING MASTER
They're what you please.

to the dancers
Hola!

ACT II

Monsieur Jourdain, Music Master, Dancing Master

M. JOURDAIN

This is none of your stupid things, and these same fellows flutter it away bravely.

MUSIC MASTER

When the dance is mixed with the music, it will have a greater effect still, and you will see something gallant in the little entertainment we have prepared for you.

M. JOURDAIN

That's however for by and by; and the person for whom I have ordered all this, is to do me the honour of dining with me here.

DANCING MASTER

Everything's ready.

MUSIC MASTER
But in short, sir, this is not enough, 'tis necessary such a person as you, who live great and have an inclination to things that are handsome, should have a concert of music at your house every Wednesday, or every Thursday.

M. JOURDAIN
Why so? Have people of quality?

MUSIC MASTER
Yes, sir.

M. JOURDAIN
I'll have one then. Will it be fine?

MUSIC MASTER
Certainly. You must have three voices, a treble, a counter-tenor, and bass, which must be accompanied with a bass-viol, a theorbo-lute, and a harpsi-chord for the thorough-bass, with two violins to play the symphonies.

M. JOURDAIN
You must add also a trumpet-marine. The trumpet-marine is an instrument that pleases me, and is very harmonious.

MUSIC MASTER
Leave us to manage matters.

M. JOURDAIN
However, don't forget by and by to send the musicians to sing at table.

MUSIC MASTER
You shall have everything you should have.

M. JOURDAIN
But above all, let the entertainment be fine.

MUSIC MASTER
You will be pleased with it, and, amongst other things, with certain minuets you will find in it.

M. JOURDAIN
Ay, the minuets are my dance; and I have a mind you should see me dance 'em. Come, master.

DANCING MASTER
Your hat, sir, if you please.

M. Jourdain takes off his foot-boy's hat, and puts it on over his own nightcap;
upon which his master takes him by the hand and makes him dance to a minuet-air
which he sings

Tol, lol, lol, lol, lol, lol,

Tol, lol, lol,

> *twice;*

Tol, lol, lol; tol, lol.

> *In time, if you please,*

Tol, lol,

> *the right leg.*

Tol, lol, lol.

> *Don't shake your shoulders so much.*

Tol, lol, lol, lol, lol.

> *Why, your arms are out of joint.*

Tol, lol, lol, lol, lol.

> *Hold up your head. Turn out your toes.*

Tol, lol, lol.

> *Your body erect.*

M. JOURDAIN
Heh?

MUSIC MASTER
Admirably well performed.

M. JOURDAIN
Now I think of it, teach me how I must bow to salute a marchioness; I shall
have occasion for it by and by.

DANCING MASTER
How you must bow to salute a marchioness?

M. JOURDAIN
Yes, a marchioness whose name is Dorimène.

DANCING MASTER
Give me your hand.

M. JOURDAIN
No. You need only to do it, I shall remember it easily.

DANCING MASTER
If you would salute her with a great deal of respect, you must first of all make a bow and fall back, then advancing towards her, bow thrice, and at the last bow down to her very knees.

M. JOURDAIN
Do it a little.
after the Dancing Master has made three bows
> Right.

*enter a Lackey
(holding two foils)*

LACKEY
Sir, your fencing master is here.

Bid him come in that he may give me a lesson.

to the Music and Dancing Masters

I'd have you stay and see me perform.

enter a Fencing Master

FENCING MASTER

taking the two foils out of the Lackey's hand, and giving one to M. Jourdain

Come, sir, your salute. Your body straight. A little bearing upon the left thigh. Your legs not so much a-straddle. Your feet both on a line. Your wrist opposite to your hip. The point of your sword over-against your shoulder. Your arm not quite so much extended. Your left hand on a level with your eye. Your left shoulder more square. Hold up your head. Your look bold. Advance. Your body steady. Beat carte, and push carte. One, two. Recover. Again with it, your foot firm. One, two. Leap back. When you make a pass, sir, 'tis necessary your sword should disengage first, and your body make as small a mark as possible. One, two. Come, beat tierce, and push the same. Advance. Your body firm. Advance. Quit after that manner. One, two. Recover. Repeat the same. One, two. Leap back. Parry, sir, parry.

the Fencing Master gives him two or three home-thrusts, crying, "Parry"

M. JOURDAIN
Ugh!

MUSIC MASTER
You do wonders.

FENCING MASTER
I have told you already—the whole secret of arms consists but in two things, in giving and not receiving. And as I showed you t'other day by demonstrative reason, it is impossible you should receive if you know how to turn your adversary's sword from the line of your body; which depends only upon a small motion of your wrist, either inward, or outward.

M. JOURDAIN
At that rate therefore, a man without any courage is sure to kill his man and not to be killed.

FENCING MASTER
Certainly. Don't you see the demonstration of it?

M. JOURDAIN
Yes.

FENCING MASTER
By this one may see of what consideration such persons as we should be esteemed in a state, and how highly the science of arms excels all the other useless sciences, such as dancing, music, and—

DANCING MASTER
Soft and fair, Monsieur *Sa, sa*. Don't speak of dancing but with respect.

MUSIC MASTER
Pray learn to treat the excellence of music in a handsomer manner.

FENCING MASTER
You're merry fellows, to pretend to compare your sciences with mine.

MUSIC MASTER

Do but see the importance of the creature!

DANCING MASTER

The droll animal there, with his leathern stomacher!

FENCING MASTER

My little master skipper, I shall make you skip as you should do. And you, my little master scraper, I shall make you sing to some tune.

DANCING MASTER

Monsieur Tick-tack, I shall teach you your trade.

M. JOURDAIN

*to the
Dancing Master*

Are you bewitched to quarrel with him, who understands tierce and carte, who knows how to kill a man by demonstrative reason?

DANCING MASTER

I laugh at his demonstrative reason, and his tierce and his carte.

M. JOURDAIN

*to the
Dancing Master*

Softly, I say.

FENCING MASTER

*to the
Dancing Master*

How? Master Impertinence!

M. JOURDAIN

Nay, my dear fencing master!

DANCING MASTER

*to the
Fencing Master*

How? You great dray-horse!

M. JOURDAIN

Nay, my dancing master.

FENCING MASTER

If I lay my—

M. JOURDAIN

to the
Fencing Master

Gently.

DANCING MASTER
If I lay my clutches on you—

M. JOURDAIN
Easily.

FENCING MASTER
I shall curry you with such an air—

M. JOURDAIN

to the
Fencing Master

For goodness' sake.

DANCING MASTER
I shall drub you after such a manner—

M. JOURDAIN

to the
Dancing Master

I beseech you.

MUSIC MASTER
Let us teach him a little how to speak.

M. JOURDAIN

to the
Music Master

Lack-a-day, be quiet.

enter a Philosophy Master

Hola, Monsieur Philosopher, you are come in the nick of time with your philosophy. Come, and make peace a little amongst these people here.

PHILOSOPHY MASTER
What's to do? What's the matter, gentlemen?

M. JOURDAIN
They have put themselves into such a passion about the preference of their professions as to call names, and would come to blows.

PHILOSOPHY MASTER

O fie, gentlemen, what need was there of all this fury? Have you not read the learned treatise upon anger, composed by Seneca? Is there anything more base and shameful than this passion, which makes a savage beast of a man? And should not reason be master of all our commotions?

DANCING MASTER

How, sir? Why he has just now been abusing us both, in despising dancing which is my employment, and music which is his profession.

PHILOSOPHY MASTER

A wise man is above all foul language that can be given him, and the grand answer one should make to all affronts is moderation and patience.

FENCING MASTER

They had both the assurance to compare their professions to mine.

PHILOSOPHY MASTER

Should this disturb you? Men should not dispute about vainglory and rank; that which perfectly distinguishes one from another is wisdom and virtue.

DANCING MASTER

I maintained to him that dancing was a science to which one cannot do sufficient honour.

MUSIC MASTER

And I, that music is one of those that all ages have revered.

FENCING MASTER

And I maintained against 'em both that the science of defence is the finest and most necessary of all sciences.

PHILOSOPHY MASTER

And what becomes of philosophy, then? You are all three very impertinent fellows, methinks, to speak with this arrogance before me; and impudently to give the name of science to things that one ought not to honour even with the name of art, that can't be comprised but under the name of a pitiful trade of gladiator, ballad-singer, and morris-dancer.

FENCING MASTER

Out, ye dog of a philosopher.

MUSIC MASTER

Hence, ye scoundrel of a pedant.

DANCING MASTER
Begone, ye arrant pedagogue.

the Philosopher falls
upon them, they all
three lay him on

PHILOSOPHY MASTER
How? Varlets as you are—

M. JOURDAIN
Monsieur Philosopher!

PHILOSOPHY MASTER
Infamous dogs! Rogues! Insolent curs!

M. JOURDAIN
Monsieur Philosopher!

FENCING MASTER
Plague on the animal!

M. JOURDAIN
Gentlemen!

PHILOSOPHY MASTER
Impudent villains!

M. JOURDAIN
Monsieur Philosopher!

DANCING MASTER
Deuce take the pack-saddled ass!

M. JOURDAIN
Gentlemen!

PHILOSOPHY MASTER
Profligate vermin!

M. JOURDAIN
Monsieur Philosopher!

MUSIC MASTER
The devil take the impertinent puppy!

M. JOURDAIN

Gentlemen!

PHILOSOPHY MASTER

Knaves! Ragamuffins! Traitors! Impostors!

M. JOURDAIN

Monsieur Philosopher! Gentlemen! Monsieur Philosopher! Gentlemen!
Monsieur Philosopher!

the four masters beat each other out

Nay, beat your hearts out if you will, I shall neither
meddle nor make with you, I shan't spoil my gown to part you. I should be
a great fool to thrust myself among them, and receive some blow that might
do me a mischief.

enter the
Philosophy Master

PHILOSOPHY MASTER

setting his band right

Now to our lesson.

M. JOURDAIN

Ah! Sir, I'm sorry for the blows they have given you.

PHILOSOPHY MASTER

'Tis nothing at all. A philosopher knows how to receive things in a proper
manner; and I'll compose a satire against 'em, in the manner of Juvenal,
that shall cut 'em most gloriously. Let that pass. What have you a mind to
learn?

M. JOURDAIN

Everything I can, for I have all the desire in the world to be a scholar, and it
vexes me that my father and mother had not made me study all the sciences
when I was young.

PHILOSOPHY MASTER

'Tis a very reasonable sentiment. *Nam, sine doctrinâ vita est quasi mortis imago.*
You understand that, and are acquainted with Latin, without doubt?

M. JOURDAIN

Yes; but act as if I were not acquainted with it. Explain me the meaning of
that.

PHILOSOPHY MASTER

The meaning of it is, that without learning, life is as it were an image of death.

M. JOURDAIN

That same Latin's in the right.

109

PHILOSOPHY MASTER
Have you not some principles, some rudiments of science?

M. JOURDAIN
Oh! yes, I can read and write.

PHILOSOPHY MASTER
Where would you please to have us begin? Would you have me teach you logic?

M. JOURDAIN
What may that same logic be?

PHILOSOPHY MASTER
It's that which teaches us the three operations of the mind.

M. JOURDAIN
What are those three operations of the mind?

PHILOSOPHY MASTER
The first, the second, and the third. The first is to conceive well, by means of universals. The second, to judge well, by means of categories. The third, to draw the conclusion right, by means of figures: Barbara, Celarent, Darii, Ferio, Baralipton, etc.

M. JOURDAIN
These words are too crabbed. This logic does not suit me by any means. Let's learn something else that's prettier.

PHILOSOPHY MASTER
Will you learn morality?

M. JOURDAIN
Morality?

PHILOSOPHY MASTER
Yes.

M. JOURDAIN
What means morality?

PHILOSOPHY MASTER
It treats of happiness, teaches men to moderate their passions, and—

M. JOURDAIN

No, no more of that. I'm as choleric as the devil, and there's no morality holds me; I will have my belly full of passion whenever I have a mind to it.

PHILOSOPHY MASTER

Would you learn physics?

M. JOURDAIN

What is it that physics treat of?

PHILOSOPHY MASTER

Physics are what explain the principles of things natural and the properties of bodies; which discourse of the nature of elements, of metals, of minerals, of stones, of plants, and animals, and teach us the cause of all the meteors; the rainbow, *ignes fatui,* comets, lightnings, thunder, thunder-bolts, rain, snow, hail, winds, and whirlwinds.

M. JOURDAIN

There's too much hurly-burly in this, too much confusion.

PHILOSOPHY MASTER

What would you have me teach you then?

M. JOURDAIN

Teach me orthography.

PHILOSOPHY MASTER

With all my heart.

M. JOURDAIN

Afterwards you may teach me the almanack, to know when there's a moon, and when not.

PHILOSOPHY MASTER

Be it so. To pursue this thought of yours right and treat this matter like a philosopher, we must begin, according to the order of things, with an exact knowledge of the nature of letters and the different manner of pronouncing them. And on this head I am to tell you that letters are divided into vowels, called vowels because they express the voice: and into consonants, so called because they sound with the vowels and only mark the different articulations of the voice. There are five vowels or voices, A, E, I, O, U.

M. JOURDAIN

I understand all that.

PHILOSOPHY MASTER

The vowel A is formed by opening the mouth very wide, A.

M. JOURDAIN
A, A. Yes.

PHILOSOPHY MASTER
The vowel E is formed by drawing the under-jaw a little nearer to the upper, A, E.

M. JOURDAIN
A, E. A, E. In troth it is. How pretty that is!

PHILOSOPHY MASTER
And the vowel I, by bringing the jaws still nearer one to the other, and stretching the two corners of the mouth towards the ears, A, E, I.

M. JOURDAIN
A, E, I, I, I, I. 'Tis true. Long live learning!

PHILOSOPHY MASTER
The vowel O is formed by re-opening the jaws and drawing the lips near at the two corners, the upper and the under, O.

M. JOURDAIN
O, O. There's nothing more just, A, E, I, O, I, O. 'Tis admirable! I, O, I, O.

PHILOSOPHY MASTER
The opening of the mouth makes exactly a little ring, which resembles an O.

M. JOURDAIN
O, O, O. You're right, O. How fine a thing it is but to know something!

PHILOSOPHY MASTER
The vowel U is formed by bringing the teeth near together without entirely joining them, and pouting out both your lips, bringing them also near together without absolutely joining 'em, U.

M. JOURDAIN
U, U. There's nothing more true, U.

PHILOSOPHY MASTER
Your two lips pout out, as if you were making faces. Whence it comes that if you would do that to anybody and make a jest of him, you need say nothing to him but U.

M. JOURDAIN

U, U. It's true. Ah! why did not I study sooner, that I might have known all this!

PHILOSOPHY MASTER

To-morrow we shall take a view of the other letters, which are the consonants.

M. JOURDAIN

Is there anything as curious in them, as in these?

PHILOSOPHY MASTER

Doubtless. The consonant D, for example, is pronounced by clapping the tip of your tongue above the upper teeth, DE.

M. JOURDAIN

DE, DE. 'Tis so. Oh! charming things! charming things!

PHILOSOPHY MASTER

The F, in leaning the upper teeth upon the lower lip, EF.

M. JOURDAIN

EF, EF. 'Tis truth. Ah! father and mother o' mine, how do I owe you a grudge!

PHILOSOPHY MASTER

And the R, in carrying the tip of the tongue up to the roof of your mouth; so that being grazed upon by the air which bursts out with a force, it yields to it, and returns always to the same part, making a kind of trill, R, ra.

M. JOURDAIN

R, r, ra. R, r, r, r, r, ra. That's true. What a clever man are you! And how have I lost time! R, r, r, ra.

PHILOSOPHY MASTER

I will explain to you all these curiosities to the bottom.

M. JOURDAIN

Pray do. But now, I must commit a secret to you. I'm in love with a person of great quality, and I should be glad you would help me to write something to her in a short *billet-doux,* which I'll drop at her feet.

PHILOSOPHY MASTER

Very well.

M. JOURDAIN

That will be very gallant, won't it?

PHILOSOPHY MASTER

Without doubt. Is it verse that you would write to her?

M. JOURDAIN
No, no, none of your verse.

PHILOSOPHY MASTER
You would only have prose?

M. JOURDAIN
No, I would neither have verse nor prose.

PHILOSOPHY MASTER
It must be one or t'other.

M. JOURDAIN
Why so?

PHILOSOPHY MASTER
Because, sir, there's nothing to express one's self by, but prose, or verse.

M. JOURDAIN
Is there nothing then but prose, or verse?

PHILOSOPHY MASTER
No, sir, whatever is not prose, is verse; and whatever is not verse, is prose.

M. JOURDAIN
And when one talks, what may that be then?

PHILOSOPHY MASTER
Prose.

M. JOURDAIN
How? When I say, Nicole, bring me my slippers, and give me my nightcap, is that prose?

PHILOSOPHY MASTER
Yes, sir.

M. JOURDAIN
On my conscience, I have spoken prose above these forty years without knowing anything of the matter; and I have all the obligations in the world to you for informing me of this. I would therefore put into a letter to her: Beautiful marchioness, your fair eyes make me die with love; but I would have this placed in a gallant manner; and have a gentle turn.

PHILOSOPHY MASTER

Why, add that the fire of her eyes has reduced your heart to ashes: that you suffer for her night and day all the torments—

M. JOURDAIN

No, no, no, I won't have all that—I'll have nothing but what I told you. Beautiful marchioness, your fair eyes make me die with love.

PHILOSOPHY MASTER

You must by all means lengthen the thing out a little.

M. JOURDAIN

No, I tell you, I'll have none but those very words in the letter: but turned in a modish way, ranged handsomely as they should be. I desire you'd show me a little, that I may see the different manners in which one may place them.

PHILOSOPHY MASTER

One may place them first of all as you said: Beautiful marchioness, your fair eyes make me die for love. Or suppose: For love die me make, beautiful marchioness, your fair eyes. Or perhaps: Your eyes fair, for love me make, beautiful marchioness, die. Or suppose: Die your fair eyes, beautiful marchioness, for love me make. Or however: Me make your eyes fair die, beautiful marchioness, for love.

M. JOURDAIN

But of all these ways, which is the best?

PHILOSOPHY MASTER

That which you said: Beautiful marchioness, your fair eyes make me die for love.

M. JOURDAIN

Yet at the same time, I never studied it, and I made the whole of it at the first touch. I thank you with all my heart, and desire you would come in good time to-morrow.

PHILOSOPHY MASTER

I shall not fail.

exit

M. JOURDAIN

to his Lackey

What? Are my clothes not come yet?

LACKEY

No, sir.

M. JOURDAIN

This cursed tailor makes me wait unreasonably, considering it's a day I have so much business in. I shall go mad. A quartan ague wring this villain of a tailor. D—l take the tailor. A plague choke the tailor. If I had him but here now, this detestable tailor, this dog of a tailor, this traitor of a tailor, I—

enter a Master Tailor and a Journeyman Tailor (bringing a suit of clothes for M. Jourdain)

Oh! You're there. I was going to be in a passion with you.

MASTER TAILOR
I could not possibly come sooner, and I set twenty fellows to work at your clothes.

M. JOURDAIN
You have sent me a pair of silk hose so tight that I had all the difficulty in the world to get 'em on, and there are two stitches broke in 'em.

MASTER TAILOR
They'll grow rather too large.

M. JOURDAIN
Yes, if I break every day a loop or two. You have made me a pair of shoes too, that pinch me execrably.

MASTER TAILOR
Not at all, sir.

M. JOURDAIN
How, not at all?

MASTER TAILOR
No, they don't pinch you at all.

M. JOURDAIN
I tell you they do hurt me.

MASTER TAILOR
You fancy so.

M. JOURDAIN
I fancy so because I feel it. There's a fine reason indeed.

MASTER TAILOR
Hold, stay, here's one of the handsomest suits at court, and the best-matched. 'Tis a masterly work to invent a grave suit of clothes that should not be black, and I'll give the cleverest tailor in town six trials to equal it.

M. JOURDAIN
What a deuce have we here? You have put the flowers downwards.

MASTER TAILOR
Why, you did not tell me you would have 'em upwards.

M. JOURDAIN
Was there any need to tell you of that?

MASTER TAILOR
Yes, certainly. All the people of quality wear 'em in that way.

M. JOURDAIN
Do people of quality wear the flowers downwards?

MASTER TAILOR
Yes, sir.

M. JOURDAIN
Oh, 'tis very well, then.

MASTER TAILOR
If you please I'll put 'em upwards.

M. JOURDAIN
No, no.

MASTER TAILOR
You need only say the word.

M. JOURDAIN
No, I tell you, you have done right. Do you think my clothes will fit me?

MASTER TAILOR
A pretty question! I defy a painter with his pencil to draw you anything that shall fit more exact. I have a fellow at home who, for fitting a pair of breeches, is the greatest genius in the world; another who, for the cut of a doublet, is the hero of the age.

M. JOURDAIN
Are the peruke and feather as they should be?

MASTER TAILOR
Everything's well.

looking earnestly at the tailor's clothes

M. JOURDAIN

Ah, hah! Monsieur Tailor, here's my stuff of the last suit you made for me. I know it very well.

MASTER TAILOR
The stuff appeared to me so handsome, that I had a mind to cut a coat out of it for myself.

M. JOURDAIN
Yes, but you should not have cabbaged it out of mine.

MASTER TAILOR
Will you put on your clothes?

M. JOURDAIN
Yes, give 'em me.

MASTER TAILOR

Stay; the matter must not go so. I have brought men along with me to dress you to music; these sort of suits are put on with ceremony. Soho? come in there, you.

enter four Journeymen Tailors, dancing

Put on this suit of the gentleman's, in the manner you do to people of quality.

two of the tailors pull off his straight breeches made for his exercises, and two others his waistcoat; then they put on his new suit to music, and M. Jourdain walks amongst them to show them his clothes to see whether they fit or no

JOURNEYMAN TAILOR

My dear gentleman, please to give the tailor's men something to drink.

M. JOURDAIN

How do you call me?

JOURNEYMAN TAILOR

My dear gentleman.

M. JOURDAIN

"My dear gentleman!" See what it is to dress like people of quality. You may go clothed like a commoner all your days, and they'll never call you "my dear gentleman."

gives them something

Stay, there's for "my dear gentleman."

JOURNEYMAN TAILOR

My lord, we are infinitely obliged to you.

M. JOURDAIN

My lord! Oh, ho! My lord! Stay, friend; "my lord" deserves something, "my lord" is none o' your petty words. Hold, there, "my lord" gives you that.

JOURNEYMAN TAILOR

My lord, we shall go drink your grace's health.

119

M. JOURDAIN

Your grace! oh, oh, oh! stay, don't go. Your grace, to me!

aside

I'faith if he goes as far as highness, he'll empty my purse.

aloud

Hold, there's for "my grace."

JOURNEYMAN TAILOR

My lord, we most humbly thank your grace for your liberality.

M. JOURDAIN

He did very well; I was going to give him all.

ACT III

Monsieur Jourdain and his two Lackeys

M. JOURDAIN

Follow me, that I may go and show my clothes a little through the town; and especially take care, both of you, to walk immediately at my heels, that people may plainly see you belong to me.

LACKEYS

Yes, sir.

M. JOURDAIN

Call me Nicole, that I may give her some directions. You need not go— here she comes.

enter Nicole

Nicole?

NICOLE
Your pleasure, sir?

M. JOURDAIN
Harkee.

laughing

NICOLE
Ha, ha, ha, ha, ha.

M. JOURDAIN
Who do ye laugh at?

NICOLE
Ha, ha, ha, ha, ha, ha.

M. JOURDAIN
What does this slut mean?

NICOLE
Ha, ha, ha. How you are bedizened! Ha, ha, ha.

M. JOURDAIN
How's that?

NICOLE
Oh! oh! my stars! ha, ha, ha, ha, ha.

M. JOURDAIN
What a jade is here! What! do ye make a jest of me?

NICOLE
No, no, sir, I should be very sorry to do so. Ha, ha, ha, ha, ha, ha.

M. JOURDAIN
I shall give ye a slap o' the chops, if you laugh any more.

NICOLE
Sir, I cannot help it. Ha, ha, ha, ha, ha, ha.

M. JOURDAIN
Won't ye have done?

NICOLE
Sir, I ask your pardon; but you are so comical, that I cannot hold from laughing. Ha, ha, ha.

M. JOURDAIN
Do but see the insolence!

NICOLE
You are so thoroughly droll there! Ha, ha.

M. JOURDAIN
I shall—

NICOLE
I beg you would excuse me. Ha, ha, ha, ha.

M. JOURDAIN
Hold, if you laugh again the least in the world, I protest and swear I'll give
ye such a box o' the ear as ye never had in your life.

NICOLE
Well, sir, I have done; I won't laugh any more.

M. JOURDAIN
Take care you don't. You must clean out against by and by—

NICOLE
Ha, ha.

M. JOURDAIN
You must clean out as it should be—

NICOLE
Ha, ha.

M. JOURDAIN
I say, you must go clean out the hall, and—

NICOLE
Ha, ha.

M. JOURDAIN
Again?

NICOLE
*tumbles down with
laughing*

Hold, sir, beat me rather, and let me laugh my belly-full, that will do me
more good. Ha, ha, ha, ha.

M. JOURDAIN
I shall run mad!

NICOLE
For goodness' sake, sir, I beseech you let me laugh. Ha, ha, ha.

M. JOURDAIN
If I take you in hand—

NICOLE
Si-ir, I shall bu-urst, if I do—not laugh. Ha, ha, ha.

M. JOURDAIN
But did ever anybody see such a jade as that, who insolently laughs in my face, instead of receiving my orders!

NICOLE
What would you have me do, sir?

M. JOURDAIN
Why, take care to get ready my house for the company that's to come by and by.

NICOLE *getting up*

Ay, i'fakins, I've no more inclination to laugh; all your company makes such a litter here that the very word's enough to put one in an ill humour.

M. JOURDAIN

What! I ought to shut my doors against all the world for your sake?

NICOLE

You ought at least to shut it against certain people.

enter Mme Jourdain

Mme JOURDAIN

Ah, hah! Here's some new story. What means this, husband, this same equipage? D'ye despise the world, that you harness yourself out in this manner? Have you a mind to make yourself a laughing-stock wherever ye go?

M. JOURDAIN

None but fools, wife, will laugh at me.

Mme JOURDAIN

In truth, people have not stayed thus long to laugh; 'tis a good while ago that your ways have furnished all the world with a laugh.

M. JOURDAIN

Who is that "all the world," pray?

Mme JOURDAIN

That "all the world" is a world perfectly in the right, and much wiser than yourself. For my part, I am shocked at the life you lead. I don't know what to call our house. One would swear 'twere carnival here all the year round; and from break o' day, for fear there should be any respite, there's nothing to be heard here but an uproar of fiddles and songsters which disturb the whole neighbourhood.

NICOLE

Madame says right. I shall never see my things set to rights again for that gang of folks that you bring to the house. They ransack every quarter of the town with their feet for dirt to bring here; and poor Frances is e'en almost slaved off her legs with scrubbing of the floors, which your pretty masters come to daub as regularly as the day comes.

M. JOURDAIN

Hey-day! our maid Nicole! you have a pretty nimble tongue of your own for a country-wench.

Mme JOURDAIN

Nicole's in the right, and she has more sense than you have. I should be glad to know what you think to do with a dancing master, at your age?

NICOLE

And with a lubberly fencing master, that comes here with his stamping to shake the whole house, and tear up all the pavement of the hall.

M. JOURDAIN

Peace, our maid, and our wife.

Mme JOURDAIN

What! will you learn to dance against the time you'll have no legs?

NICOLE

What! have you a mind to murder somebody?

M. JOURDAIN

Hold your prate; I tell you you are ignorant creatures, both of you, and don't know the advantage of all this.

Mme JOURDAIN

You ought much rather to think of marrying your daughter, who is of age to be provided for.

M. JOURDAIN

I shall think of marrying my daughter when a suitable match presents itself; but I shall think too of learning the *belles sciences*.

NICOLE

I've heard say further, madame, that to pin the basket, he has got him a philosophy master to-day.

M. JOURDAIN

Very well. I've a mind to have wit, and to know how to reason upon things with your genteel people.

Mme JOURDAIN

Won't you go to school one of these days, and be whipped at your age?

M. JOURDAIN

Why not? Would I were whipped this very instant before all the world, so I did but know what they learn at school!

NICOLE

Yes, forsooth, that would be a mighty advantage t'ye.

M. JOURDAIN

Without doubt.

Mme JOURDAIN

This is all very necessary to the management of your house.

M. JOURDAIN

Certainly. You talk, both of you, like asses, and I'm ashamed of your ignorance.

to Mme Jourdain

For example, do you know, you, what it is you now speak?

Mme JOURDAIN

Yes, I know that what I speak is very right, and that you ought to think of living in another manner.

M. JOURDAIN

I don't talk of that. I ask you what the words are that you now speak?

Mme JOURDAIN

They are words that have a good deal of sense in them, and your conduct is by no means such.

M. JOURDAIN

I don't talk of that, I tell you. I ask you, what is that I now speak to you, which I say this very moment?

Mme JOURDAIN

Mere stuff.

M. JOURDAIN

Pshaw, no, 'tis not that. That which we both of us say, the language we speak this instant?

Mme JOURDAIN

Well?

M. JOURDAIN
How is it called?

Mme JOURDAIN
'Tis called just what you please to call it.

M. JOURDAIN
'Tis prose, you ignorant creature.

Mme JOURDAIN
Prose?

M. JOURDAIN
Yes, prose. Whatever is prose, is not verse; and whatever is not verse, is prose. Now, see what it is to study. And you,
to Nicole
do you know very well how you must do to say U?

NICOLE
How?

M. JOURDAIN
Yes. What is it you do when you say U?

NICOLE
What?

M. JOURDAIN
Say U a little, to try.

NICOLE
Well, U.

M. JOURDAIN
What is it you do?

NICOLE
I say U.

M. JOURDAIN
Yes, but when you say U, what is it you do?

NICOLE
I do as you bid me.

M. JOURDAIN
O! what a strange thing it is to have to do with brutes! You pout out your lips, and bring your under-jaw to your upper, U, d'ye see? I make a mouth, U.

NICOLE
Yes, that's fine.

Mme JOURDAIN
'Tis admirable!

M. JOURDAIN
'Tis quite another thing, had but you seen O, and DE, DE, and EF, EF.

Mme JOURDAIN
What is all this ridiculous stuff?

NICOLE
What are we the better for all this?

M. JOURDAIN

It makes one mad, to see these ignorant women.

Mme JOURDAIN

Go, go, you should send all these folks apacking with their silly stuff.

NICOLE

And especially that great lubberly fencing master, who fills all my house with dust.

M. JOURDAIN

Hey-day! This fencing master sticks strangely in thy stomach. I'll let thee see thy impertinence presently.

he orders the foils to be brought, and gives one to Nicole

Stay, reason demonstrative, the line of the body. When they push in carte one need only do so; and when they push in tierce one need only do so. This is the way never to be killed; and is not that clever to be upon sure grounds, when one has an encounter with any-body? There, push at me a little, to try.

NICOLE

Well, how?

Nicole gives him several thrusts

M. JOURDAIN

Gently! Hold! Oh! Softly; deuce take the hussy.

NICOLE

You bid me push.

M. JOURDAIN

Yes, but you push me in tierce before you push in carte, and you have not patience while I parry.

Mme JOURDAIN

You are a fool, husband, with all these whims, and this is come to you since you have taken upon you to keep company with quality.

M. JOURDAIN

When I keep company with quality, I show my judgment; and that's much better than herding with your bourgeoisie.

Mme JOURDAIN

Yes, truly, there's a great deal to be got by frequenting your nobility; and you have made fine work with that count you are so bewitched with.

M. JOURDAIN

Peace, take care what you say. Do you well know, wife, that you don't know whom you speak of when you speak of him? He's a man of more importance than you think of; a nobleman of consideration at court, who speaks to the king just for all the world as I speak to you. Is it not a thing that does me great honour, that you see a person of that quality come so often to my house, who calls me his dear friend and treats me as if I were his equal? He has more kindness for me than one would ever imagine, and he caresses me in such a manner before all the world that I myself am perfectly confounded at it.

Mme JOURDAIN

Yes, he has a great kindness for you, and caresses you; but he borrows your money of you.

M. JOURDAIN

Well, and is it not a great honour to me to lend money to a man of that condition? And can I do less for a lord who calls me his dear friend?

Mme JOURDAIN

And what is it this lord does for you?

M. JOURDAIN

Things that would astonish you if you did but know 'em.

Mme JOURDAIN

And what may they be?

M. JOURDAIN

Peace, I can't explain myself. 'Tis sufficient that if I have lent him money, he'll pay it me honestly, and that before 'tis long.

Mme JOURDAIN

Yes, stay you for that.

M. JOURDAIN

Certainly. Did he not tell me so?

Mme JOURDAIN

Yes, yes, and he won't fail to disappoint you.

M. JOURDAIN

He swore to me on the faith of a gentleman.

Mme JOURDAIN

A mere song.

M. JOURDAIN

Hey! You are mighty obstinate, wife of mine; I tell you he will keep his word with me, I am sure of it.

Mme JOURDAIN

And I am sure that he will not, and all the court he makes to you is only to cajole you.

M. JOURDAIN

Hold your tongue. Here he comes.

Mme JOURDAIN

That's all we shall have of him. He comes perhaps to borrow something more of you; the very sight of him gives me my dinner.

M. JOURDAIN

Hold your tongue, I say.

enter Dorante

DORANTE

My dear friend, Monsieur Jourdain, how do you do?

M. JOURDAIN

Very well, sir, to do you what little service I can.

DORANTE

And Madame Jourdain there, how does she do?

Mme JOURDAIN

Madame Jourdain does as well as she can.

DORANTE

Hah! Monsieur Jourdain, you're dressed the most genteelly in the world!

M. JOURDAIN

As you see.

DORANTE

You have a very fine air with that dress, and we have ne'er a young fellow at court that's better made than you.

M. JOURDAIN

He, he.

Mme JOURDAIN *aside*

He scratches him where it itches.

DORANTE

Turn about. 'Tis most gallant.

Mme JOURDAIN *aside*

Yes, as much of the fool behind as before.

DORANTE

'Faith, Monsieur Jourdain, I was strangely impatient to see you. You're the man in the world I most esteem, and I was talking of you again this morning at the king's levee.

M. JOURDAIN

You do me a great deal of honour, sir.

to Mme Jourdain

At the king's levee!

DORANTE

Come, be covered.

M. JOURDAIN

Sir, I know the respect I owe you.

DORANTE

Lack-a-day, be covered; no ceremony, pray, between us two.

M. JOURDAIN

Sir—

DORANTE

Put on your hat, I tell you, Monsieur Jourdain; you are my friend.

M. JOURDAIN

Sir, I am your humble servant.

DORANTE

I won't be covered, if you won't.

133

puts on his hat

M. JOURDAIN

I choose rather to be unmannerly than troublesome.

DORANTE

I am your debtor, you know.

aside

Mme JOURDAIN

Yes, we know it but too well.

DORANTE

You have generously lent me money upon several occasions; and have obliged me, most certainly, with the best grace in the world.

M. JOURDAIN

You jest, sir.

DORANTE

But I know how to repay what is lent me, and to be grateful for the favours done me.

M. JOURDAIN

I don't doubt it, sir.

DORANTE

I'm willing to get out of your books, and came hither to make up our accounts together.

aside to
Mme Jourdain

M. JOURDAIN

Well, you see your impertinence, wife.

DORANTE

I'm one who love to be out of debt as soon as I can.

aside to
Mme Jourdain

M. JOURDAIN

I told you so.

DORANTE

Let's see a little what 'tis I owe you.

134

M. JOURDAIN *aside to Mme Jourdain*

You there, with your ridiculous suspicions.

DORANTE

Do you remember right all the money you have lent me?

M. JOURDAIN

I believe so. I made a little memorandum of it. Here it is. Let you have at one time two hundred louis d'or.

DORANTE

'Tis true.

M. JOURDAIN

Another time, six-score.

DORANTE

Yes.

M. JOURDAIN

And another time a hundred and forty.

DORANTE

You are right.

M. JOURDAIN

These three articles make four hundred and sixty louis d'or, which come to five thousand and sixty livres.

DORANTE

The account is very right. Five thousand and sixty livres.

M. JOURDAIN

One thousand eight hundred and thirty-two livres to your plume-maker.

DORANTE

Just.

M. JOURDAIN

Two thousand seven hundred and four-score livres to your tailor.

DORANTE

'Tis true.

M. JOURDAIN

Four thousand three hundred and seventy-nine livres, twelve sols, and eight deniers to your tradesman.

DORANTE

Very well. Twelve sols, eight deniers. The account is just.

M. JOURDAIN

And a thousand seven hundred and forty-eight livres, seven sols, four deniers to your saddler.

DORANTE

'Tis all true. What does that come to?

M. JOURDAIN

Sum total, fifteen thousand eight hundred livres.

DORANTE

The sum total, and just. Fifteen thousand and eight hundred livres. To which add two hundred pistoles, which you are going to lend me, that will make exactly eighteen thousand francs, which I shall pay you the first opportunity.

aside to M. Jourdain

Mme JOURDAIN

Well, did I not guess how 'twould be!

aside to Mme Jourdain

M. JOURDAIN

Peace.

DORANTE

Will it incommode you to lend me what I tell you?

M. JOURDAIN
Oh! no.

aside to M. Jourdain

Mme JOURDAIN

This man makes a mere milch cow of you.

aside to Mme Jourdain

M. JOURDAIN

Hold your tongue.

DORANTE
If this will incommode you, I'll seek it elsewhere.

M. JOURDAIN
No, sir.

Mme JOURDAIN   *aside to M. Jourdain*
He'll ne'er be satisfied till he has ruined you.

M. JOURDAIN   *aside to Mme Jourdain*
Hold your tongue, I tell you.

DORANTE
You need only tell me if this puts you to any straits.

M. JOURDAIN
Not at all, sir.

Mme JOURDAIN   *aside to M. Jourdain*
'Tis a true wheedler.

M. JOURDAIN   *aside to Mme Jourdain*
Hold your tongue then.

Mme JOURDAIN   *aside to M. Jourdain*
He'll drain you to the last farthing.

M. JOURDAIN   *aside to Mme Jourdain*
Will you hold your tongue?

DORANTE
I've a good many people would be glad to lend it me, but as you are my very good friend, I thought I should wrong you if I asked it of anybody else.

M. JOURDAIN

'Tis too much honour, sir, you do me. I'll go fetch what you want.

*aside to
M. Jourdain*

Mme JOURDAIN

What! going to lend him still more?

*aside to
Mme Jourdain*

M. JOURDAIN

What can I do? Would you have me refuse a man of that rank, who spoke of me this morning at the king's levee?

*aside to
M. Jourdain*

Mme JOURDAIN

Go, you're a downright dupe.

exit M. Jourdain

DORANTE

You seem to me very melancholy. What ails you, Madame Jourdain?

Mme JOURDAIN

My head's bigger than my fist, even if it is not swelled.

DORANTE

Where is Mademoiselle your daughter that I don't see her?

Mme JOURDAIN

Mademoiselle my daughter is pretty well where she is.

DORANTE

How does she go on?

Mme JOURDAIN

She goes on her two legs.

DORANTE

Won't you come with her, one of these days, and see the ball, and the play that's acted at court?

Mme JOURDAIN

Yes, truly, we've a great inclination to laugh, a great inclination to laugh have we.

DORANTE

I fancy, Madame Jourdain, you had a great many sparks in your younger years, being so handsome and good-humoured as you were.

Mme JOURDAIN

Tredame, sir! what, is Madame Jourdain grown decrepit, and does her head totter already with a palsy?

DORANTE

Odso, Madame Jourdain, I ask your pardon. I was not thinking that you are young. I'm very often absent. Pray excuse my impertinence.

*enter
M. Jourdain*

M. JOURDAIN

to Dorante

Here's two hundred pieces for you, hard money.

DORANTE

I do assure you, Monsieur Jourdain, I am absolutely yours; and I long to do you service at court.

M. JOURDAIN

I'm infinitely obliged to you.

DORANTE

If Madame Jourdain inclines to see the royal diversion, I'll get her the best places in the ballroom.

Mme JOURDAIN

Madame Jourdain kisses your hand.

DORANTE

*aside to
M. Jourdain*

Our pretty marchioness, as I informed you in my letter, will be here by and by to partake of your ball and collation; I brought her, at last, to consent to the entertainment you design to give her.

M. JOURDAIN

Let us draw to a distance a little, for a certain reason.

DORANTE

'Tis eight days since I saw you, and I gave you no tidings of the diamond you put into my hands to make her a present of, as from you; but the reason was, I had all the difficulty in the world to conquer her scruples, and 'twas no longer ago than to-day, that she resolved to accept of it.

M. JOURDAIN
How did she like it?

DORANTE
Marvellously; and I am much deceived if the beauty of this diamond has not an admirable effect upon her.

M. JOURDAIN
Grant it, kind Heaven!

to Nicole **Mme JOURDAIN**
When he's once with him, he can never get rid of him.

DORANTE
I made her sensible in a proper manner of the richness of the present and the strength of your passion.

M. JOURDAIN
These kindnesses perfectly overwhelm me; I am in the greatest confusion in the world to see a person of your quality demean himself on my account as you do.

DORANTE
You jest sure. Does one ever stop at such sort of scruples among friends? And would not you do the same thing for me, if occasion offered?

M. JOURDAIN
Oh! certainly, and with all my soul.

aside to Nicole **Mme JOURDAIN**
How the sight of him torments me!

DORANTE
For my part, I never mind anything when a friend is to be served; and when you imparted to me the ardent passion you had entertained for the agreeable marchioness, with whom I was acquainted, you see that I made an immediate offer of my service.

M. JOURDAIN
'Tis true, these favours are what confound me.

140

Mme JOURDAIN *to Nicole*

What! will he never be gone?

NICOLE

They are mighty great together.

DORANTE

You've taken the right way to smite her. Women, above all things, love the expense we are at on their account; and your frequent serenades, your continual entertainments, that sumptuous firework she saw on the water, the diamond she received by way of present from you, and the regale you are now preparing—all this speaks much better in favour of your passion than all the things you yourself could possibly have said to her.

M. JOURDAIN

There's no expense I would not be at, if I could by that means find the way to her heart. A woman of quality has powerful charms for me, and 'tis an honour I would purchase at any rate.

Mme JOURDAIN *aside to Nicole*

What can they have to talk of so long together? Go softly, and listen a little.

DORANTE

By and by you will enjoy the pleasure of seeing her at your ease; your eyes will have full time to be satisfied.

M. JOURDAIN

To be at full liberty, I have ordered matters so that my wife shall dine with my sister, where she'll pass the whole afternoon.

DORANTE

You have done wisely, for your wife might have perplexed us a little. I have given the proper orders for you to the cook, and for everything necessary for the ball. 'Tis of my own invention; and provided the execution answers the plan, I am sure 'twill be—

M. JOURDAIN *perceives that Nicole listens, and gives her a box on the ear*

Hey, you're very impertinent.

to Dorante

Let us go if you please.

exeunt
M. Jourdain
and Dorante

NICOLE

I'faith, curiosity has cost me something; but I believe there's a snake in the grass, for they were talking of some affair which they were not willing you should be present at.

Mme JOURDAIN

This is not the first time, Nicole, that I have had suspicions of my husband. I am the most deceived person in the world, or there is some amour in agitation, and I am labouring to discover what it should be. But let's think of my daughter. You know the love Cléonte has for her. He is a man who hits my fancy, and I have a mind to favour his addresses and help him to Lucile, if I can.

NICOLE

In truth, madame, I am the most ravished creature in the world, to find you in these sentiments; for if the master hits your taste, the man hits mine no less; and I could wish our marriage might be concluded under favour of theirs.

Mme JOURDAIN

Go, and talk with him about it, as from me, and tell him to come to me presently, that we may join in demanding my daughter of my husband.

NICOLE

I fly, madame, with joy, and I could not have received a more agreeable commission.

exit Mme Jourdain

I believe I shall very much rejoice their hearts.

enter Cléonte and Covielle

Hah, most luckily met. I'm an ambassadress of joy, and I come—

CLÉONTE

Be gone, ye perfidious slut, and don't come to amuse me with thy traitorous speeches.

NICOLE

Is it thus you receive—

CLÉONTE

Be gone, I tell thee, and go directly and inform thy false mistress, that she never more, while she lives, shall impose upon the too simple Cléonte.

NICOLE

What whim is this? My dear Covielle, tell me a little what does this mean.

COVIELLE

Thy dear Covielle, wicked minx? Away quickly out of my sight, hussy, and leave me at quiet.

NICOLE

What! dost thou, too—

COVIELLE

Out o' my sight, I tell thee, and talk not to me, for thy life.

NICOLE *aside*

Hey-day! What gadfly has stung 'em both? Well, I must march and inform my mistress of this pretty piece of history. *exit*

CLÉONTE

What! treat a lover in this manner; and a lover the most constant, the most passionate of all lovers!

COVIELLE

'Tis a horrible trick they have served us both.

CLÉONTE

I discover all the ardour for her, all the tenderness one can imagine. I love nothing in the world but her, have nothing in my thoughts besides her. She is all my care, all my desire, all my joy. I speak of nought but her, think of nought but her, dream of nought but her, I breathe only for her, my heart lives wholly in her; and this is the worthy recompense of such a love! I am two days without seeing her, which are to me two horrible ages; I meet her accidentally, my heart feels all transported at the sight; joy sparkles in my face; I fly to her with ecstasy, and the faithless creature turns away her eyes, and brushes hastily by me, as if she had never seen me in her life!

COVIELLE

I say the same as you do.

CLÉONTE

Is it possible to see anything, Covielle, equal to this perfidy of the ungrateful Lucile?

COVIELLE

Or to that, sir, of the villainous jade Nicole?

CLÉONTE

After so many ardent sacrifices of sighs and vows that I have made to her charms!

COVIELLE

After so much assiduous sneaking, cares, and services that I have paid her in the kitchen!

CLÉONTE

So many tears that I have shed at her feet!

COVIELLE

So many buckets of water that I have drawn for her!

CLÉONTE

Such ardour as I have shown, in loving her more than myself!

COVIELLE

So much heat as I have endured, in turning the spit in her place!

CLÉONTE

She flies me with disdain!

COVIELLE

She turns her back upon me with impudence!

CLÉONTE

This is a perfidy worthy the greatest punishment.

COVIELLE

This a treachery that deserves a thousand boxes o' the ear.

CLÉONTE

Prithee, never think to speak once more to me in her favour.

COVIELLE

I, sir? Marry, Heaven forbid.

CLÉONTE

Never come to excuse the action of this perfidious woman.

COVIELLE

Fear it not.

CLÉONTE

No, d'ye see, all discourses in her defence will signify nothing.

COVIELLE

Who dreams of such a thing?

CLÉONTE

I'm determined to continue my resentment against her, and break off all correspondence.

COVIELLE

I give my consent.

CLÉONTE

This same count that visits her, pleases perhaps her eye; and her fancy, I see plainly, is dazzled with quality. But I must, for my own honour, prevent the triumph of her inconstancy. I'll make as much haste as she can do towards the change which I see she's running into, and won't leave her all the glory of quitting me.

COVIELLE

'Tis very well said, and for my share, I enter into all your sentiments.

CLÉONTE

Second my resentments, and support my resolutions against all the remains of love that may yet plead for her. I conjure thee, say all the ill things of her thou canst. Paint me her person so as to make her despicable; and, in order to disgust me, mark me out well all the faults thou canst find in her.

COVIELLE

She, sir? A pretty mawkin, a fine piece to be so much enamoured with. I see nothing in her but what's very indifferent, and you might find a hundred persons more deserving of you. First of all she has little eyes.

CLÉONTE

That's true, she has little eyes; but they are full of fire, the most sparkling, the most piercing in the world, the most striking that one shall see.

145

COVIELLE
She has a wide mouth.

CLÉONTE
Yes; but one sees such graces in it, as one does not see in other mouths, and the sight of that mouth inspires desire: 'tis the most attractive, the most amorous in the world.

COVIELLE
As to her height, she's not tall.

CLÉONTE
No; but she's easy, and well-shaped.

COVIELLE
She affects a negligence in speaking and acting.

CLÉONTE
'Tis true; but all this has a gracefulness in her, and her ways are engaging; they have I don't know what charms that insinuate into our hearts.

COVIELLE
As to her wit—

CLÉONTE
Ah! Covielle, she has the most refined, the most delicate turn of wit.

COVIELLE
Her conversation—

CLÉONTE
Her conversation is charming.

COVIELLE
She's always grave.

CLÉONTE
Would you have flaunting pleasantry, a perpetual profuse mirth? And d'ye see anything more impertinent than those women who are always upon the giggle?

COVIELLE
But in short, she is the most capricious creature in the world.

CLÉONTE

Yes, she is capricious, I grant ye, but everything sits well upon fine women; we bear with everything from the fair.

COVIELLE

Since that's the case, I see plainly you desire always to love her.

CLÉONTE

I! I should love death sooner; and I am now going to hate her as much as ever I loved her.

COVIELLE

But how, if you think her so perfect?

CLÉONTE

Therein shall my vengeance be more glaring; therein shall I better display the force of my resolution in hating her, quitting her, most beautiful as she is; most charming, most amiable, as I think her. Here she is.

enter Lucile and Nicole

NICOLE   *to Lucile*

For my part, I was perfectly shocked at it.

LUCILE

It can be nothing else, Nicole, but what I said. But there he comes.

CLÉONTE   *to Covielle*

I won't so much as speak to her.

COVIELLE

I'll follow your example.

LUCILE

What means this, Cléonte, what's the matter with you?

NICOLE

What ails thee, Covielle?

LUCILE

What trouble has seized you?

147

NICOLE
What cross humour possesses thee?

LUCILE
Are you dumb, Cléonte?

NICOLE
Hast thou lost thy speech, Covielle?

CLÉONTE
The abandoned creature!

COVIELLE
Oh! the Judas!

LUCILE
I see very well that the late meeting has disordered your mind.

CLÉONTE *to Covielle*

O, ho! She sees what she has done.

NICOLE

The reception of this morning has made thee take snuff.

COVIELLE *to Cléonte*

She has guessed where the shoe pinches.

LUCILE

Is it not true, Cléonte, that this is the reason of your being out of humour?

CLÉONTE

Yes, perfidious maid, that is it, since I must speak; and I can tell you that you shall not triumph, as you imagine, by your unfaithfulness, that I shall be beforehand in breaking with you, and you won't have the credit of discarding me. I shall, doubtless, have some difficulty in conquering the passion I have for you: 'twill cause me uneasiness; I shall suffer for a while; but I shall compass my point, and I would sooner stab myself to the heart than have the weakness of returning to you.

COVIELLE *to Nicole*

As says the master, so says the man.

LUCILE

Here's a noise indeed about nothing. I'll tell you, Cléonte, the reason that made me avoid joining you this morning.

CLÉONTE *endeavouring to go to avoid Lucile*

No, I'll hear nothing.

NICOLE *to Covielle*

I'll let thee into the cause that made us pass you so quick.

COVIELLE *endeavouring to go to avoid Nicole*

I will hear nothing.

LUCILE *following Cléonte*

Know that this morning—

149

walks about without regarding Lucile

CLÉONTE

No, I tell you.

following Covielle

NICOLE

Learn that—

walks about likewise without regarding Nicole

COVIELLE

No, traitress.

LUCILE
Hear me.

CLÉONTE
Not a bit.

NICOLE
Let me speak.

COVIELLE
I'm deaf.

LUCILE
Cléonte!

CLÉONTE
No.

NICOLE
Covielle!

COVIELLE
No.

LUCILE
Stay.

CLÉONTE
Idle stuff.

NICOLE
Hear me.

150

COVIELLE
No such thing.

LUCILE
One moment.

CLÉONTE
Not at all.

NICOLE
A little patience.

COVIELLE
A fiddle-stick.

LUCILE
Two words.

CLÉONTE
No, 'tis over.

NICOLE
One word.

COVIELLE
No more dealings.

LUCILE *stopping*
Well, since you won't hear me, keep your opinion, and do what you please.

NICOLE *stopping likewise*
Since that's thy way, e'en take it all just as it pleases thee.

CLÉONTE
Let's know the subject then of this fine reception.

LUCILE *going in her turn to avoid Cléonte*
I've no longer an inclination to tell it.

COVIELLE
Let us a little into this history.

NICOLE

going likewise in her turn to avoid Covielle

I won't inform thee now, not I.

CLÉONTE

following Lucile

Tell me—

LUCILE

No, I'll tell you nothing.

COVIELLE

following Nicole

Say—

NICOLE

No, I say nothing.

CLÉONTE

For goodness' sake.

LUCILE

No, I tell you.

COVIELLE

Of all charity.

NICOLE

Not a bit.

CLÉONTE

I beseech you.

LUCILE

Let me alone.

COVIELLE

I conjure thee.

NICOLE

Away with thee.

CLÉONTE

Lucile!

LUCILE

No.

COVIELLE

Nicole!

NICOLE

Not at all.

CLÉONTE

For Heaven's sake.

LUCILE

I will not.

COVIELLE

Speak to me.

NICOLE

Not a word.

CLÉONTE

Clear up my doubts.

LUCILE

No, I'll do nothing towards it.

COVIELLE

Cure my mind.

NICOLE

No, 'tis not my pleasure.

CLÉONTE

Well, since you are so little concerned to ease me of my pain, and to justify yourself as to the unworthy treatment my passion has received from you, ungrateful creature, 'tis the last time you shall see me, and I am going far from you to die of grief and love.

COVIELLE

And I'll follow his steps.   *to Nicole*

LUCILE   *to Cléonte, who is going*

Cléonte!

to Covielle, who
follows his master

NICOLE

Covielle!

stopping

CLÉONTE

Hey?

likewise stopping

COVIELLE

Your pleasure?

LUCILE

Whither do you go?

CLÉONTE

Where I told you.

COVIELLE

We go to die.

LUCILE

Do you go to die, Cléonte?

CLÉONTE

Yes, cruel, since you will have it so.

LUCILE

I? I have you die?

CLÉONTE

Yes, you would.

LUCILE

Who told you so?

going up to Lucile

CLÉONTE

Would you not have it so, since you would not clear up my suspicions?

LUCILE

Is that my fault? Would you but have given me the hearing, should I not have told you that the adventure you make such complaints about was occasioned this morning by the presence of an old aunt who will absolutely have it that the mere approach of a man is a dishonour to a girl, who is perpetually lecturing us upon this head, and represents to us all mankind as so many devils, whom one ought to avoid.

NICOLE *to Covielle*

There's the whole secret of the affair.

CLÉONTE

Don't you deceive me, Lucile?

COVIELLE *to Nicole*

Dost thou not put a trick upon me?

LUCILE *to Cléonte*

There's nothing more true.

NICOLE *to Covielle*

'Tis the very thing, as it is.

COVIELLE *to Cléonte*

Shall we surrender upon this?

CLÉONTE

Ah, Lucile, what art have you to calm my passions with a single word! How easily do we suffer ourselves to be persuaded by those we love!

COVIELLE

How easily is one wheedled by these plaguy animals!

enter Mme Jourdain

Mme JOURDAIN

I am very glad to see you, Cléonte, and you are here apropos. My husband's acoming; catch your opportunity quick, and demand Lucile in marriage.

CLÉONTE

Ah, madame, how sweet is that word, how it flatters my wishes! Could I

receive an order more charming? a favour more precious?

enter M. Jourdain

Sir, I was not willing to employ any other person to make a certain demand of you which I have long intended. It concerns me sufficiently to undertake it in my own person; and, without farther circumlocution, I shall inform you that the honour of being your son-in-law is an illustrious favour which I beseech you to grant me.

M. JOURDAIN

Before I give you an answer, sir, I desire you would tell me whether you are a gentleman.

CLÉONTE

Sir, the generality of people don't hesitate much on this question. People speak out bluff, and with ease. They make no scruple of taking this title upon 'em, and custom now-a-days seems to authorise the theft. For my part, I confess to you, my sentiments in this matter are somewhat more delicate.

156

I look upon all imposture as unworthy an honest man, and that there is cowardice in denying what Heaven has made us; in tricking ourselves out, to the eyes of the world, in a stolen title; in desiring to put ourselves off for what we are not. I am undoubtedly born of parents who have held honourable employments. I have had the honour of six years' service in the army; and I find myself of consequence enough to hold a tolerable rank in the world; but for all this I won't give myself a name, which others in my place would think they might pretend to, and I'll tell you frankly that I am no gentleman.

M. JOURDAIN

Your hand, sir; my daughter is no wife for you.

CLÉONTE

How?

M. JOURDAIN

You are no gentleman, you shan't have my daughter.

Mme JOURDAIN

What would you be at then with your gentlemen? D'ye think we sort of people are of the line of St. Louis?

M. JOURDAIN

Hold your tongue, wife, I see you're acoming.

Mme JOURDAIN

Are we either of us otherwise descended than of plain citizens?

M. JOURDAIN

There's a scandalous reflection for you!

Mme JOURDAIN

And was not your father a tradesman as well as mine?

M. JOURDAIN

Plague take the woman! She never has done with this. If your father was a tradesman, so much was the worse for him; but as for mine, they are numskulls that say he was. All that I have to say to you is that I will have a gentleman for my son-in-law.

Mme JOURDAIN

Your daughter should have a husband that's proper for her, and an honest man who is rich and well made would be much better for her than a gentleman who is deformed and a beggar.

NICOLE

That's very true. We have a young squire in our town who is the most awkward looby, the veriest driveller that I ever set eyes on.

M. JOURDAIN

Hold your prate, Madame Impertinence. You are always thrusting yourself into conversation. I've means sufficient for my daughter, and want nothing but honour, and I will have her a marchioness.

Mme JOURDAIN

A marchioness!

M. JOURDAIN

Yes, a marchioness.

Mme JOURDAIN

Marry, Heaven preserve me from it!

M. JOURDAIN

'Tis a determined thing.

Mme JOURDAIN

'Tis what I shall never consent to. Matches with people above one are always subject to grievous inconveniences. I don't like that a son-in-law should have it in his power to reproach my daughter with her parents, or that she should have children who should be ashamed to call me grandmother. Should she come and visit me with the equipage of a grand lady and, through inadvertency, miss curtsying to some of the neighbourhood, they would not fail, presently, saying a hundred idle things. Do but see, would they say, this lady marchioness, what haughty airs she gives herself! She's the daughter of Monsieur Jourdain, who was over and above happy, when she was a little one, to play children's play with us. She was not always so lofty as she is now; and her two grandfathers sold cloth near St. Innocent's Gate. They amassed great means for their children, which they are paying for now, perhaps very dear, in the other world. People don't generally grow so rich by being honest. I won't have all these tittle-tattle stories; in one word, I'll have a man who shall be beholden to me for my daughter, and to whom I can say, Sit you down there, son-in-law, and dine with me.

M. JOURDAIN

See there the sentiments of a little soul, to desire always to continue in a mean condition. Let me have no more replies; my daughter shall be a marchioness in spite of the world; and if you put me in a passion, I'll make her a duchess.

exit

158

Mme JOURDAIN

Cléonte, don't be discouraged by all this.

to Lucile

Follow me, daughter, and come tell your father resolutely that if you have not him, you won't marry anybody at all.

exeunt
Mme Jourdain
Lucile, and Nicole

COVIELLE

You have made a pretty piece of work of it with your fine sentiments.

CLÉONTE

What wouldst thou have me do? I have a scrupulousness in this case that no precedents can conquer.

COVIELLE

You're in the wrong to be serious with such a man as that. Don't you see that he's a fool? And would it cost you anything to accommodate yourself to his chimeras?

CLÉONTE

You're in the right; but I did not dream it was necessary to bring your proofs of nobility, to be son-in-law to Monsieur Jourdain.

COVIELLE *laughing*

Ha, ha, ha.

CLÉONTE

What d'ye laugh at?

COVIELLE

At a thought that's come into my head to play our spark off and help you to obtain what you desire.

CLÉONTE

How?

COVIELLE

The thought is absolutely droll.

CLÉONTE

What is it?

159

COVIELLE

There was a certain masquerade performed a little while ago, which comes in here the best in the world; and which I intend to insert into a piece of roguery I design to make for our coxcomb. This whole affair looks a little like making a joke of him; but with him we may hazard everything. There's no need here to study finesse so much—he's a man who will play his part to a wonder, and will easily give in to all the sham tales we shall take in our heads to tell him. I have actors, I have habits all ready, only let me alone.

CLÉONTE

But inform me of it.

COVIELLE

I am going to let you into the whole of it. Let's retire; there he comes.

exeunt
Covielle and Cléonte
enter
M. Jourdain

M. JOURDAIN

What a deuce can this mean? They have nothing but great lords to reproach me with; and I for my part see nothing so fine as keeping company with your great lords; there's nothing but honour and civility among 'em, and I would it had cost me two fingers of a hand to have been born a count or a marquis.

enter a Lackey

LACKEY

Sir, here's the count, and a lady whom he's handing in.

M. JOURDAIN

Good lack-a-day, I have some orders to give. Tell 'em that I'm acoming in a minute.

exit
M. Jourdain
enter Dorante
and Dorimène

LACKEY

My master says that he's acoming in a minute.

exit Lackey

DORANTE

'Tis very well.

DORIMÈNE

I don't know, Dorante; I take a strange step here in suffering you to bring me to a house where I know nobody.

160

DORANTE

What place then, madame, would you have a lover choose to entertain you in, since, to avoid clamour, you neither allow of your own house nor mine?

DORIMÈNE

But you don't mention that I am every day insensibly engaged to receive too great proofs of your passion. In vain do I refuse things, you weary me out of resistance, and you have a civil kind of obstinacy which makes me come gently into whatsoever you please. Frequent visits commenced, declarations came next, which drew after them serenades and entertainments, which were followed by presents. I opposed all these things, but you are not disheartened, and you become master of my resolutions step by step. For my part, I can answer for nothing hereafter, and I believe in the end you will bring me to matrimony, from which I stood so far aloof.

DORANTE

Faith, madame, you ought to have been there already. You are a widow, and depend upon nobody but yourself. I am my own master, and love you more than my life. What does it stick at, then, that you should not, from this day forward, complete my happiness?

DORIMÈNE

Lack-a-day, Dorante, there must go a great many qualities on both sides, to make people live happily together; and two of the most reasonable persons in the world have often much ado to compose a union to both their satisfactions.

DORANTE

You're in the wrong, madame, to represent to yourself so many difficulties in this affair; and the experience you have had concludes nothing for the rest of the world.

DORIMÈNE

In short, I always abide by this. The expenses you put yourself to for me disturb me for two reasons; one is, they engage me more than I could wish; and the other is, I'm sure (no offence to you!) that you can't do this but you must incommode yourself, and I would not have you do that.

DORANTE

Fie, madame, these are trifles, and 'tis not by that—

DORIMÈNE

I know what I say; and, amongst other things, the diamond you forced me to take, is of value—

161

DORANTE

Nay, madame, pray don't enhance the value of a thing my love thinks unworthy of you: and permit—Here's the master of the house.

*enter
M. Jourdain*

*after having made two
bows, finding himself
too near Dorimène*

M. JOURDAIN

A little farther, madame.

DORIMÈNE

How?

M. JOURDAIN

One step, if you please.

DORIMÈNE

What then?

M. JOURDAIN

Fall back a little for the third.

DORANTE

Monsieur Jourdain, madame, knows the world.

M. JOURDAIN

Madame, 'tis a very great honour that I am fortunate enough to be so happy, but to have the felicity that you should have the goodness to grant me the favour, to do me the honour, to honour me with the favour of your presence; and had I also the merit to merit a merit like yours, and that Heaven— envious of my good—had granted me—the advantage of being worthy —of—

DORANTE

Monsieur Jourdain, enough of this; my lady does not love great compliments, and she knows you are a man of wit.

aside to Dorimène

'Tis a downright bourgeois, ridiculous enough, as you see, in his whole behaviour.

DORIMÈNE   *aside to Dorante*

It is not very difficult to perceive it.

DORANTE

Madame, this is a very good friend of mine.

M. JOURDAIN

'Tis too much honour you do me.

DORANTE

A very polite man.

DORIMÈNE

I have a great esteem for hïm.

M. JOURDAIN

I have done nothing yet, madame, to merit this favour.

DORANTE   *aside to M. Jourdain*

Take good care however not to speak to her of the diamond you gave her.

M. JOURDAIN   *aside to Dorante*

Mayn't I ask her only how she likes it?

DORANTE

aside to M. Jourdain

How! Take special care you don't. 'Twould be villainous of you; and to act like a man of gallantry, you should make as if it were not you who made the present.

aloud

Monsieur Jourdain, madame, says that he's in raptures to see you at his house.

DORIMÈNE

He does me a great deal of honour.

M. JOURDAIN

aside to Dorante

How am I obliged to you, sir, for speaking to her in that manner on my account!

DORANTE

aside to M. Jourdain

I have had a most terrible difficulty to get her to come hither.

M. JOURDAIN

aside to Dorante

I don't know how to thank you enough for it.

DORANTE

He says, madame, that he thinks you the most charming person in the world.

DORIMÈNE

'Tis a great favour he does me.

M. JOURDAIN

Madame, it's you who do the favours, and—

DORANTE

Let's think of eating.

enter a Lackey

LACKEY

to M. Jourdain

Everything is ready, sir.

DORANTE

Come, then, let us sit down to table; and fetch the musicians.

ACT IV

Dorimène, Monsieur Jourdain, Dorante, three Musicians, Lackeys

DORIMÈNE

How, Dorante? Why here's a most magnificent repast!

M. JOURDAIN

You are pleased to banter, madame; I would it were more worthy of your acceptance.

Dorimène,
M. Jourdain, Dorante,
and three Musicians sit
down at the table

DORANTE

Monsieur Jourdain, madame, is in the right in what he says, and he obliges me in paying you, after so handsome a manner, the honours of his house. I agree with him that the repast is not worthy of you. As it was myself who ordered it, and I am not so clearly sighted in these affairs as certain of our friends, you have here no very learned feast; and you will find incongruities of good cheer in it, some barbarisms of good taste. Had our friend Damis had a hand here, everything had been done by rule; elegance and erudition would have run through the whole, and he would not have failed exaggerating all the regular pieces of the repast he gave you, and force you to own his great capacity in the science of good eating; he would have told you of bread *de rive,* with the golden kissing-crust, raised too all round with a crust that crumples tenderly in your teeth; of wine with a velvet sap, heightened with a smartness not too overpowering; of a breast of mutton stuffed with parsley; of a loin of veal *de rivière,* thus long, white, delicate, and which is a true almond paste between the teeth; of your partridges heightened with a surprising *goût*; and then by way of farce or entertainment, of a soup with jelly broth, fortified with a young plump turkey-pout, cantoned with pigeons, and garnished with white onions married to succory. But, for my part, I confess to you my ignorance; and, as Monsieur Jourdain has very well said, I wish the repast were more worthy of your acceptance.

DORIMÈNE

I make no other answer to this compliment than eating as I do.

M. JOURDAIN

Ah! what pretty hands are there!

DORIMÈNE

The hands are so so, Monsieur Jourdain; but you mean to speak of the diamond, which is very pretty.

M. JOURDAIN

I, madame? Marry, Heaven forbid I should speak of it; I should not act like a gentleman of gallantry, and the diamond is a very trifle.

DORIMÈNE

You are wondrous nice.

M. JOURDAIN

You have too much goodness—

DORANTE

having made signs to M. Jourdain

Come, give some wine to Monsieur Jourdain, and to those gentlemen who will do us the favour to sing us a catch.

DORIMÈNE

You give a wondrous relish to the good cheer by mixing music with it; I am admirably well regaled here.

M. JOURDAIN

Madame, it is not—

DORANTE

Monsieur Jourdain, let us listen to these gentlemen, they'll entertain us with something better than all we can possibly say.

First and Second MUSICIANS

together, each with a glass in his hand

Put it round, my dear Phyllis, invert the bright glass;
  Oh what charms to the crystal those fingers impart!
You and Bacchus combined, all resistance surpass,
  And with passion redoubled have ravished my heart.
    'Twixt him, you, and me, my charmer, my fair,
    Eternal affection let's swear.

At the touch of those lips how he sparkles more bright!
And his touch, in return, those lips does embellish:
I could quaff 'em all day, and drink bumpers all night.
What longing each gives me, what gusto, what relish!
'Twixt him, you, and me, my charmer, my fair,
Eternal affection let's swear.

Second and Third MUSICIANS

together

Since time flies so nimbly away,
Come drink, my dear boys, drink about;
Let's husband him well while we may,
For life may be gone before the mug's out.
When Charon has got us aboard,
Our drinking and wooing are past;
We ne'er to lose time can afford,
For drinking's a trade not always to last.

Let your puzzling rogues in the schools,
Dispute of the bonum *of man;*
Philosophers dry are but fools—
The secret is this: drink, drink off your can.
When Charon has got us aboard,
Our drinking and wooing are past;
We ne'er to lose time can afford,
For drinking's a trade not always to last.

ALL THREE

together

Why bob there! some wine, boys! come fill the glass, fill,
Round and round let it go, till we bid it stand still.

DORIMÈNE

I don't think anything can be better sung; and 'tis extremely fine.

M. JOURDAIN

I see something here though, madame, much finer.

DORIMÈNE

Hey! Monsieur Jourdain is more gallant than I thought he was.

DORANTE

How, madame! who do you take Monsieur Jourdain for?

M. JOURDAIN

I wish she would take me for what I could name.

DORIMÈNE

Again?

DORANTE

You don't know him.   *to Dorimène*

M. JOURDAIN

She shall know me whenever she pleases.

DORIMÈNE

Oh! Too much.

DORANTE

He's one who has a repartee always at hand. But you don't see, madame, that Monsieur Jourdain eats all the pieces you have touched.

DORIMÈNE

Monsieur Jourdain is a man that I am charmed with.

M. JOURDAIN

If I could charm your heart, I should be—

enter
Mme Jourdain

Mme JOURDAIN

Hey-day! why here's a jolly company of you, and I see very well you did not expect me. It was for this pretty affair, then, Monsieur Husband o' mine, that you were in such a violent hurry to pack me off to dine with my sister; I just now found a play-house below, and here I find a dinner fit for a wedding. Thus it is you spend your money, and thus it is you feast the ladies in my absence, and present 'em with music and a play, whilst I'm sent abroad in the meantime.

DORANTE

What do you mean, Madame Jourdain? and what's your fancy to take it into your head that your husband spends his money, and that 'tis he who entertains my lady? Know, pray, that 'tis I do it, that he only lends me his house, and that you ought to consider a little better what you say.

M. JOURDAIN

Yes, Madame Impertinence, 'tis the count that presents the lady with all

169

this, who is a person of quality. He does me the honour to borrow my house, and is pleased to let me be with him.

Mme JOURDAIN

'Tis all stuff, this. I know what I know.

DORANTE

Madame Jourdain, take your best spectacles, take 'em.

Mme JOURDAIN

I've no need of spectacles, sir, I see clear enough; I've smelt things out a great while ago, I am no ass. 'Tis base in you, who are a great lord, to lend a helping hand, as you do, to the follies of my husband. And you, madame, who are a great lady, 'tis neither handsome nor honest in you to sow dissension in a family, and to suffer my husband to be in love with you.

DORIMÈNE

What can be the meaning of all this? Go, Dorante, 'tis wrong in you to expose me to the silly visions of this raving woman.

DORANTE

following Dorimène, who goes out

Madame, why madame, where are you running?

M. JOURDAIN

Madame—My lord, make my excuses to her and endeavour to bring her back.

exit Dorante   *to Mme Jourdain*

Ah! impertinent creature as you are, these are your fine doings; you come and affront me in the face of all the world, and drive people of quality away from my house.

Mme JOURDAIN

I value not their quality.

Lackeys take away the table

M. JOURDAIN

I don't know what hinders me, you plaguy hussy, from splitting your skull with the fragments of the feast you came here to disturb.

Mme JOURDAIN

going

I despise all this. I defend my own rights, and I shall have all the wives on my side.

M. JOURDAIN

You do well to get out of the way of my fury.

exit Mme Jourdain

She came here at a most un-
lucky time. I was in the humour of saying fine things, and never did I find
myself so witty. What have we got here?

*enter Covielle,
disguised*

COVIELLE

Sir, I don't know whether I have the honour to be known to you.

M. JOURDAIN

No, sir.

COVIELLE

I have seen you when you were not above thus tall.

M. JOURDAIN

Me?

COVIELLE

Yes. You were one of the prettiest children in the world; and all the ladies
used to take you in their arms to kiss you.

M. JOURDAIN

To kiss me?

COVIELLE

Yes, I was an intimate friend of the late gentleman your father.

M. JOURDAIN

Of the late gentleman my father!

COVIELLE

Yes. He was a very honest gentleman.

M. JOURDAIN

What is't you say?

COVIELLE

I say that he was a very honest gentleman.

M. JOURDAIN

My father?

COVIELLE

Yes.

M. JOURDAIN
Did you know him very well?

COVIELLE
Certainly.

M. JOURDAIN
And did you know him for a gentleman?

COVIELLE
Without doubt.

M. JOURDAIN
I don't know then what the world means.

COVIELLE
How?

M. JOURDAIN
There is a stupid sort of people who would face me down that he was a tradesman.

COVIELLE
He a tradesman? 'Tis mere scandal; he never was one. All that he did was, that he was very obliging, very officious, and as he was a great connoisseur in stuffs, he used to pick them up everywhere, have 'em carried to his house, and gave 'em to his friends for money.

M. JOURDAIN
I'm very glad of your acquaintance, that you may bear witness that my father was a gentleman.

COVIELLE
I'll maintain it in the face of all the world.

M. JOURDAIN
You will oblige me. What business brings you here?

COVIELLE
Since my acquaintance with the late gentleman your father, honest gentleman, as I was telling you, I have travelled round the world.

M. JOURDAIN
Round the world?

COVIELLE
Yes.

M. JOURDAIN
I fancy 'tis a huge way off, that same country.

COVIELLE
Most certainly. I have not been returned from these tedious travels of mine but four days. And because I have an interest in everything that concerns you, I come to tell you the best news in the world.

M. JOURDAIN
What?

COVIELLE
You know that the son of the Great Turk is here.

M. JOURDAIN
I? No.

COVIELLE
How? He has a most magnificent train. All the world goes to see him, and he has been received in this country as a person of importance.

M. JOURDAIN
In troth, I did not know that.

COVIELLE
What is of advantage to you in this affair is that he is in love with your daughter.

M. JOURDAIN
The son of the Great Turk?

COVIELLE
Yes, and wants to be your son-in-law.

M. JOURDAIN
My son-in-law, the son of the Great Turk?

COVIELLE

The son of the Great Turk your son-in-law. As I have been to see him, and perfectly understand his language, he held a conversation with me; and after some other discourse, says he to me: "Acciam croc soler, onch alla moustaph gidelum amanahem varahini oussere carbulath." That is to say, "Have you not seen a young handsome person, who is the daughter of Monsieur Jourdain, a gentleman of Paris?"

M. JOURDAIN

The son of the Great Turk said that of me?

COVIELLE

Yes, as I made answer to him that I knew you particularly well, and that I had seen your daughter. Ah, says he to me, "Marababa sahem"; that is to say, "Ah! how am I enamoured with her!"

M. JOURDAIN

"Marababa sahem" means: "Ah! how am I enamoured with her"?

COVIELLE

Yes.

M. JOURDAIN

Marry, you did well to tell me so, for as for my part, I should never have believed that "Marababa sahem" had meant, "Ah! how am I enamoured with her!" 'Tis an admirable language, this same Turkish!

COVIELLE

More admirable than one can believe. Do you know very well what is the meaning of "Cacaramouchen"?

M. JOURDAIN

"Cacaramouchen"? No.

COVIELLE

'Tis as if you should say, "My dear soul."

M. JOURDAIN

"Cacaramouchen" means, "My dear soul"?

COVIELLE

Yes.

174

M. JOURDAIN

Why, 'tis very wonderful! "Cacaramouchen—my dear soul." Would one ever have thought it? I am perfectly confounded at it.

COVIELLE

In short, to finish my embassy, he comes to demand your daughter in marriage; and to have a father-in-law who should be suitable to him, he designs to make you a Mamamouchi, which is a certain grand dignity of his country.

M. JOURDAIN

Mamamouchi?

COVIELLE

Yes, Mamamouchi; that is to say, in our language, a Paladin. Paladin is your ancient—Paladin, in short—there's nothing in the world more noble than this; and you will rank with the grandest lord upon earth.

M. JOURDAIN

The son of the Great Turk does me a great deal of honour, and I desire you would carry me to him, to return him my thanks.

COVIELLE

How? Why he's just acoming hither.

M. JOURDAIN

Is he acoming hither?

COVIELLE

Yes. And he brings all things along with him for the ceremony of your dignity.

M. JOURDAIN

He's main hasty.

COVIELLE

His love will suffer no delay.

M. JOURDAIN

All that perplexes me, in this case, is that my daughter is an obstinate hussy who has took into her head one Cléonte, and vows she'll marry no person besides him.

COVIELLE

She'll change her opinion when she sees the son of the Grand Turk; and then there happens here a very marvellous adventure, that is, that the son

175

of the Grand Turk resembles this Cléonte, with a trifling difference. I just now came from him, they showed him me; and the love she bears for one may easily pass to the other, and—I hear him coming; there he is.

enter Cléonte, like a Turk, and three Pages holding up his gown

CLÉONTE
Ambousahim oqui boraf, Iordina, salamalequi.

to M. Jourdain

COVIELLE
That is to say, Monsieur Jourdain, "May your heart be all the year like a rose-tree in flower!" These are obliging ways of speaking in that country.

M. JOURDAIN
I am His Turkish Highness's most humble servant.

COVIELLE
Carigar camboto oustin moraf.

CLÉONTE
Oustin yoc catamalequi basum base alla moran.

COVIELLE
He says, "Heaven give you the strength of lions and the prudence of serpents!"

M. JOURDAIN
His Turkish Highness does me too much honour; and I wish him all manner of prosperity.

COVIELLE
Ossa binamin sadoc babally oracaf ouram.

CLÉONTE
Bel-men.

COVIELLE
He says that you should go quickly with him to prepare yourself for the ceremony, in order afterwards to see your daughter and to conclude the marriage.

M. JOURDAIN
So many things in two words?

COVIELLE

Yes, the Turkish language is much in that way; it says a great deal in a few words. Go quickly where he desires you.

exeunt M. Jourdain, Cléonte, and Pages

Ha, ha, ha. I'faith, this is all absolutely droll. What a dupe! Had he had his part by heart, he could not have played it better. O, ho!

enter Dorante

I beseech you, sir, lend us a helping hand here, in a certain affair which is in agitation.

DORANTE

Ah! ah! Covielle, who could have known thee? How art thou trimmed out there!

COVIELLE

You see, ha, ha!

DORANTE

What do ye laugh at?

COVIELLE

At a thing, sir, that well deserves it.

DORANTE

What?

COVIELLE

I could give you a good many times, sir, to guess the stratagem we are making use of with Monsieur Jourdain, to bring him over to give his daughter to my master.

DORANTE

I don't at all guess the stratagem, but I guess it will not fail of its effect, since you undertake it.

COVIELLE

I know, sir, you are not unacquainted with the animal.

DORANTE

Tell me what it is.

COVIELLE

Be at the trouble of withdrawing a little farther off, to make room for what I see acoming. You will see one part of the story whilst I give you a narration of the rest.

THE TURKISH CEREMONY

The Mufti, Dervishes, Turks (assisting the Mufti), Singers and Dancers

Six Turks enter gravely, two and two, to the sound of instruments. They bear three carpets, with which they dance in several figures, and then lift them up very high. The Turks, singing, pass under the carpets and range themselves on each side of the stage. The Mufti, accompanied by Dervishes, closes the march.

Then the Turks spread the carpets on the ground and kneel down upon them, the Mufti and the Dervishes standing in the middle of them; while the Mufti invokes Mahomet in dumb contortions and grimaces, the Turks prostrate themselves to the ground, singing Allah, *raising their hands to heaven, singing* Allah, *and so continuing alternately to the end of the invocation, when they all rise up, singing* Allahekber.

Then two Dervishes bring Monsieur Jourdain, clothed like a Turk, his head shaved, without a turban or sabre.

MUFTI

to M. Jourdain

If thou understandest,
* Answer;*
If thou dost not understand,
* Hold thy peace, hold thy peace.*

I am Mufti,
* Thou! who thou art*
I don't know :
* Hold thy peace, hold thy peace.*

two Dervishes retire
with M. Jourdain

Say, Turk, who is this,
An Anabaptist, an Anabaptist?

THE TURKS
No.

MUFTI
A Zwinglian?

THE TURKS
No.

MUFTI
A Coffite?

THE TURKS
No.

MUFTI
A Hussite? A Morist? A Fronist?

THE TURKS
No, no, no.

MUFTI
No, no, no. Is he a Pagan?

THE TURKS
No.

MUFTI
A Lutheran?

THE TURKS
No.

MUFTI
A Puritan?

THE TURKS
No.

MUFTI
A Brahmin? A Moffian? A Zurian?

THE TURKS
No, no, no.

MUFTI
No, no, no. A Mahometan, a Mahometan?

THE TURKS
There you have it, there you have it.

MUFTI
How is he called? How is he called?

THE TURKS
Jourdain, Jourdain.

dancing

MUFTI
Jourdain! Jourdain!

THE TURKS
Jourdain, Jourdain.

MUFTI

> To Mahomet for Jourdain
> I pray night and day,
> That he would make a Paladin
> Of Jourdain, of Jourdain.
> Give him a turban, and give a sabre,
> With a galley and a brigantine,
> To defend Palestine.
> To Mahomet for Jourdain
> I pray night and day.

to the Turks

Is Jourdain a good Turk?

THE TURKS
That he is, that he is.

singing and dancing

MUFTI

> Ha, la ba, ba la chou, ba la ba, ba la da.

exit

THE TURKS

> Ha, la ba, ba la chou, ba la ba, ba la da.

The Mufti returns with the State Turban, which is of an immeasurable largeness, garnished with lighted wax candles, four or five rows deep, accompanied by two Dervishes, bearing the Alcoran, with comic caps garnished also with lighted candles.

182

The two other Dervishes lead up Monsieur Jourdain and place him on his knees with his hands to the ground so that his back, on which the Alcoran is placed, may serve for a desk to the Mufti, who makes a second burlesque invocation, knitting his eyebrows, striking his hands sometimes upon the Alcoran, and tossing over the leaves with precipitation, after which, lifting up his hands, and crying with a loud voice, Hoo.

During this second invocation the assistant Turks, bowing down and raising themselves alternately, sing likewise,

HOO, HOO, HOO.

M. JOURDAIN

after they have taken the Alcoran off his back

Ouf!

MUFTI

to M. Jourdain

Thou wilt not be a knave?

THE TURKS

No, no, no.

MUFTI

Not be a thief?

THE TURKS

No, no, no.

MUFTI

to the Turks

Give the turban.

THE TURKS

Thou wilt not be a knave?
No, no, no.
Not be a thief?
No, no, no.
Give the turban.

the Turks, dancing, put the turban on M. Jourdain's head at the sound of the instruments

183

giving the sabre to
M. Jourdain

MUFTI

> *Be brave, be no scoundrel,*
> *Take the sabre.*

drawing their sabres

THE TURKS

> *Be brave, be no scoundrel,*
> *Take the sabre.*

the Turks, dancing,
strike M. Jourdain
several times
with their sabres,
to music

MUFTI

> *Give, give*
> *The bastonade.*

THE TURKS

> *Give, give*
> *The bastonade.*

the Turks, dancing,
give M. Jourdain
several strokes with
a cudgel, to music

MUFTI

> *Don't think it a shame,*
> *This is the last affront.*

THE TURKS

> *Don't think it a shame,*
> *This is the last affront.*

The Mufti begins a third invocation. The Dervishes support him with great respect, after which the Turks, singing and dancing round the Mufti, retire with him and lead off Monsieur Jourdain.

ACT V

Madame Jourdain, Monsieur Jourdain

Bless us all! Mercy upon us! What have we got here? What a figure! What! dressed to go a-mumming, and is this a time to go masked? Speak therefore, what does this mean? Who has trussed you up in this manner?

M. JOURDAIN
Do but see the impertinent slut, to speak after this manner to a Mamamouchi.

Mme JOURDAIN
How's that?

M. JOURDAIN
Yes, you must show me respect now I am just made a Mamamouchi.

Mme JOURDAIN
What d'ye mean with your Mamamouchi?

M. JOURDAIN
Mamamouchi, I tell you. I am a Mamamouchi.

Mme JOURDAIN
What beast is that?

M. JOURDAIN
Mamamouchi, that is to say, in our language, a Paladin.

Mme JOURDAIN
A Paladin? Are you of an age to be a morris-dancer?

M. JOURDAIN
What an ignoramus! I say, Paladin. 'Tis a dignity of which I have just now gone through the ceremony.

Mme JOURDAIN
What ceremony then?

M. JOURDAIN
Mahameta per Jordina.

Mme JOURDAIN
What does that mean?

M. JOURDAIN
Jordina, that is to say, Jourdain.

Mme JOURDAIN
Well, how Jourdain?

M. JOURDAIN
Voler far un Paladina de Jordina.

Mme JOURDAIN
What?

M. JOURDAIN
Dar turbanta con galera.

Mme JOURDAIN
What's the meaning of that?

M. JOURDAIN
Per deffender Palestina.

Mme JOURDAIN

What is it you would say?

M. JOURDAIN

Dara, dara, bastonnara.

Mme JOURDAIN

What is this same jargon?

M. JOURDAIN

Non tener honta, questa star l'ultima affronta.

Mme JOURDAIN

What in the name of wonder can all this be?

M. JOURDAIN

singing and dancing

Hou la ba, ba la chou, ba la ba, ba la da.

falls down to the ground

Mme JOURDAIN

Alas and well-a-day! My husband is turned fool.

M. JOURDAIN

getting up and walking off

Peace! insolence, show respect to Monsieur Mamamouchi.

Mme JOURDAIN

alone

How could he lose his senses? I must run and prevent his going out.

seeing Dorimène and Dorante

So, so,

here come the rest of our gang. I see nothing but vexation on all sides.

exit Mme Jourdain enter Dorante and Dorimène

DORANTE

Yes, madame, you'll see the merriest thing that can be seen; and I don't believe it's possible, in the whole world, to find another man so much a fool as this here. And besides, madame, we must endeavour to promote Cléonte's amour and to countenance his masquerade. He's a very pretty gentleman and deserves that one should interest one's self in his favour.

DORIMÈNE

I've a very great value for him, and he deserves good fortune.

DORANTE

Besides, we have here, madame, an entertainment that will suit us, and which we ought not to suffer to be lost; and I must by all means see whether my fancy will succeed.

DORIMÈNE

I saw there magnificent preparations, and these are things, Dorante, I can no longer suffer. Yes, I'm resolved to put a stop, at last, to your profusions; and to break off all the expenses you are at on my account, I have determined to marry you out of hand. This is the real secret of the affair, and all these things end, as you know, with marriage.

DORANTE

Ah! madame, is it possible you should form so kind a resolution in my favour?

DORIMÈNE

I only do it to prevent you from ruining yourself; and without this, I see plainly that before 'tis long you won't be worth a groat.

DORANTE

How am I obliged to you, madame, for the care you take to preserve my estate! 'Tis entirely at your service, as well as my heart, and you may use both of 'em just in the manner you please.

DORIMÈNE

I shall make a proper use of them both. But here comes your man; an admirable figure.

enter
M. Jourdain

DORANTE

Sir, my lady and I are come to pay our homage to your new dignity, and to rejoice with you at the marriage you are concluding betwixt your daughter and the son of the Grand Turk.

M. JOURDAIN

bowing first in the
Turkish manner

Sir, I wish you the force of serpents and the wisdom of lions.

DORIMÈNE

I was exceeding glad to be one of the first, sir, who should come and congratulate you upon the high degree of glory to which you are raised.

M. JOURDAIN

Madame, I wish your rose-tree may flower all the year round; I am infinitely obliged to you for interesting yourselves in the honour that's paid me; and I am greatly rejoiced to see you returned hither, that I may make my most humble excuses for the impertinence of my wife.

DORIMÈNE

That's nothing at all, I can excuse a commotion of this kind in her; your heart ought to be precious to her, and 'tis not at all strange the possession of such a man as you are should give her some alarms.

M. JOURDAIN

The possession of my heart is a thing you have entirely gained.

DORANTE

You see, madame, that Monsieur Jourdain is none of those people whom prosperity blinds, and that he knows, in all his grandeur, how to own his friends.

DORIMÈNE

'Tis the mark of a truly generous soul.

DORANTE

Where is His Turkish Highness? We should be glad, as your friends, to pay our devoirs to him.

M. JOURDAIN

There he comes, and I have sent to bring my daughter to join hands with him.

enter Cléonte, in a Turkish habit

DORANTE

to Cléonte

Sir, we come to compliment Your Highness, as friends of the gentleman your father-in-law, and to assure you, with respect, of our most humble services.

M. JOURDAIN

Where's the dragoman, to tell him who you are and make him understand what you say? You shall see that he'll answer you, and he speaks Turkish marvellously. Hola! there; where the deuce is he gone?

to Cléonte

Stref,
strif,
strof,
straf.

The gentleman is a

grande segnore, grande segnore, grande segnore;

and madame is a

granda dama, granda dama.

seeing he cannot make himself be understood

Lack-a-day!

to Cléonte

Sir, he be a French
Mamamouchi, and madame a French Mamamouchess. I can't speak plainer.
Good, here's the dragoman.

enter Covielle, disguised

Where do you run? We can say nothing without you.

pointing to Cléonte

Inform him a little that the gentleman and lady are persons of great
quality who come to pay their compliments to him, as friends of mine, and
to assure him of their services.

to Dorimène and Dorante

You shall see how he will answer.

COVIELLE

Alabala crociam, acci boram alabamen.

CLÉONTE

Catalequi tubal ourin soter amalouchan.

M. JOURDAIN

to Dorimène and Dorante

Do ye see?

COVIELLE

He says that the rain of prosperity waters, at all seasons, the garden of your
family.

M. JOURDAIN

I told you that he speaks Turkish.

DORANTE

This is admirable.

enter Lucile

M. JOURDAIN

Come, daughter, come nearer, and give the gentleman your hand who does
you the honour of demanding you in marriage.

LUCILE

What's the matter, father, how are you dressed here? What! are you playing a comedy?

M. JOURDAIN

No, no, 'tis no comedy, 'tis a very serious affair; and the most honourable for you that possibly can be wished.

pointing to Cléonte

This is the husband I bestow upon you.

LUCILE

Upon me, father?

M. JOURDAIN

Yes, upon you. Come, take him by the hand, and thank Heaven for your good fortune.

LUCILE

I won't marry.

M. JOURDAIN

I'll make you; am I not your father?

LUCILE

I won't do it.

M. JOURDAIN

Here's a noise indeed! Come, I tell you. Your hand here.

LUCILE

No, father, I've told you before that there's no power can oblige me to take any other husband than Cléonte; and I am determined upon all extremities rather than—

discovering Cléonte

'Tis true that you are my father; I owe you absolute obedience; and you may dispose of me according to your pleasure.

M. JOURDAIN

Hah, I am charmed to see you return so readily to your duty; and it is a pleasure to me to have my daughter obedient.

enter Mme Jourdain

Mme JOURDAIN

How, how, what does this mean? They tell me you design to marry your daughter to a mummer.

191

M. JOURDAIN

Will you hold your tongue, impertinence? You're always coming to mix
your extravagances with everything; there's no possibility of teaching you
common sense.

Mme JOURDAIN

'Tis you whom there's no teaching to be wise, and you go from folly to folly.
What's your design, what would you do with this flock of people?

M. JOURDAIN

I design to marry my daughter to the son of the Grand Turk.

Mme JOURDAIN

To the son of the Grand Turk?

M. JOURDAIN

Yes.

pointing to Covielle

Make your compliments to him by the dragoman there.

Mme JOURDAIN

I have nothing to do with the dragoman, and I shall tell him plainly to his face that he shall have none of my daughter.

M. JOURDAIN

Will you hold your tongue once more?

DORANTE

What, Madame Jourdain, do you oppose such an honour as this? Do you refuse His Turkish Highness for a son-in-law?

Mme JOURDAIN

Lack-a-day, sir, meddle you with your own affairs.

DORIMÈNE

'Tis a great honour, 'tis by no means to be rejected.

Mme JOURDAIN

Madame, I desire you too not to give yourself any trouble about what no ways concerns you.

DORANTE

'Tis the friendship we have for you that makes us interest ourselves in what is of advantage to you.

Mme JOURDAIN

I shall easily excuse your friendship.

DORANTE

There's your daughter consents to her father's pleasure.

Mme JOURDAIN

My daughter consent to marry a Turk?

DORANTE

Certainly.

Mme JOURDAIN

Can she forget Cléonte?

DORANTE
What would one not do to be a great lady?

Mme JOURDAIN
I would strangle her with my own hands, had she done such a thing as this.

M. JOURDAIN
Here's tittle-tattle in abundance. I tell you this marriage shall be consummated.

Mme JOURDAIN
And I tell you that it shall not be consummated.

M. JOURDAIN
What a noise is here?

LUCILE
Mother!

Mme JOURDAIN
Go, you are a pitiful hussy.

to Mme Jourdain **M. JOURDAIN**
What! do you scold her for being obedient to me?

Mme JOURDAIN
Yes, she belongs to me as well as you.

to Mme Jourdain **COVIELLE**
Madame.

Mme JOURDAIN
What would you say to me, you?

COVIELLE
One word.

Mme JOURDAIN
I've nothing to do with your word.

to M. Jourdain **COVIELLE**
Sir, would she hear me but one word in private, I'll promise you to make her consent to what you have a mind.

Mme JOURDAIN
I won't consent to it.

COVIELLE
Only hear me.

Mme JOURDAIN
No.

M. JOURDAIN   *to Mme Jourdain*
Give him the hearing.

Mme JOURDAIN
No, I won't hear him.

M. JOURDAIN
He'll tell you—

Mme JOURDAIN
He shall tell me nothing.

M. JOURDAIN
Do but see the great obstinacy of the woman! Will it do you any harm to hear him?

COVIELLE
Only hear me; you may do what you please afterwards.

Mme JOURDAIN
Well, what?

COVIELLE   *aside to
                                    Mme Jourdain*
We have made signs to you, madame, this hour. Don't you see plainly that all is done purely to accommodate ourselves to the visions of your husband; that we are imposing upon him under this disguise, and that it is Cléonte himself who is the son of the Great Turk?

Mme JOURDAIN   *aside to Covielle*
Oh, oh?

195

COVIELLE

aside to
Mme Jourdain

And that 'tis me, Covielle, who am the dragoman?

Mme JOURDAIN

aside to Covielle

Oh! in that case, I give up.

COVIELLE

aside to
Mme Jourdain

Don't seem to know anything of the matter.

Mme JOURDAIN

aloud

Yes, 'tis all done, I consent to the marriage.

M. JOURDAIN

Ay, all the world submits to reason.

to Madame Jourdain

You would not hear him. I knew he would explain to you what the son of the Great Turk is.

Mme JOURDAIN

He has explained it to me sufficiently, and I'm satisfied with it. Let us send for a notary.

DORANTE

'Tis well said. And, Madame Jourdain, that you may set your mind perfectly at rest, and that you should this day quit all jealousy which you may have entertained of the gentleman your husband, my lady and I shall make use of the same notary to marry us.

Mme JOURDAIN

I consent to that too.

M. JOURDAIN

aside to Dorante

'Tis to make her believe.

DORANTE

aside to
M. Jourdain

We must by all means amuse her a little with this pretence.

196

M. JOURDAIN

Good, good.

aloud

Let somebody go for the notary.

DORANTE

In the meantime, till he comes and has drawn up the contracts, let us see our entertainment, and give His Turkish Highness the diversion of it.

M. JOURDAIN

Well advised; come let us take our places.

Mme JOURDAIN

And Nicole?

M. JOURDAIN

I give her to the dragoman; and my wife, to whosoever pleases to take her.

COVIELLE

Sir, I thank you.

aside

If it's possible to find a greater fool than this, I'll go and publish it in Rome.